Is Brazil Afraid of the World?

Is Brazil Afraid of the World?
Discussing Brazilian Foreign Affairs and Challenges

Roberto Teixeira da Costa

December 2022

ANTHEM PRESS

Anthem Press
An imprint of Wimbledon Publishing Company
www.anthempress.com

This edition first published in UK and USA 2023
by ANTHEM PRESS
75–76 Blackfriars Road, London SE1 8HA, UK
or PO Box 9779, London SW19 7ZG, UK
and
244 Madison Ave #116, New York, NY 10016, USA

British Library Cataloguing-in-Publication Data
A catalogue record for this book is available from the British Library.

Library of Congress Control Number: 2023900042
A catalog record for this book has been requested.

ISBN-13: 978-1-83998-747-2 (Pbk)
ISBN-10: 1-83998-747-2 (Pbk)

Cover Credit: ALIA3

This title is also available as an e-book.

AFFAIRS AND CHALLENGES

The Brazil Institute at King's College London was lucky to benefit from the expertise and experience of Roberto Teixeira da Costa when he was a visitor with us in 2018. Roberto used his visitorship in London to start the production of this book. This is a provocative analysis, not only of Brazil's foreign policy, but of its political economy and role in the global economy. Anyone who believes that Brazil could and should play a more influential role in world affairs will benefit from reading this book

Dr. Anthony Pereira

Professor, Director, Kimberly Green Latin American and Caribbean Center at FIU and Former Director, Brazil Institute and Department of International Development, School of Global Affairs, King's College London

SUMMARY

INTRODUCTION

ROBERTO TEIXEIRA DA COSTA

My book in Portuguese—*O Brasil tem medo do mundo? Ou o mundo tem medo do Brasil?*—was launched by Editora Noeses in 2021. After the official release a videoconference was held with different personalities, among them Anthony Pereira, at that time the head of the Brazilian Institute of King's College London, who suggested an English version of the book.

At first, I did not give much attention to this possibility. I was fully dedicated to promoting my book in Brazil in different media and conferences with no time to think about it. Also, that effort was higher than usual due to the Covid-19 pandemic, because there were no "book signings" in person to promote it.

As time passed, I began to consider the possibility. I spoke with Vinicius Carvalho, a professor at King's College who introduced me to Anthem Press. My motivation to explore this possibility was the fact that my book, among other issues, discussed the lack of knowledge about Brazil internationally, be it in academia, business or in the press.

After the initial contact, Anthem Press indicated their willingness to publish the book. Then the process started, and it proved to be much more complex and time consuming than I initially imagined.

I was not familiar with the process of editing a book outside Brazil, which in my specific case implied adjusting it to Anthem Press specifications, quite different and more detailed than in Brazil.

A deeper commitment was required, and I gradually had to adjust to the procedures recommended. At Anthem Press, also, there were several people involved, each from a different area. As time passed it became obvious that we were dealing with much more than a translation. Peer review produced excellent considerations to better adapt it for the English reader. Also, during this adjustment period I came to the conclusion that it was fundamental to adjust the book to new realities that emerged in the world in the last two years and their consequences for Brazil. Also, in October 2022 a presidential election was held in Brazil. Thus, the return of Luiz Inácio Lula da Silva to the presidency for the third time implied a possible radical change in foreign policies that were being implemented by Jair Bolsonaro in his four-year term.

In international politics, the war in Ukraine and its consequences for the world required additional consideration.

In adapting the book to these new realities, several parts were eliminated since they had lost relevance and ability to impact the future.

Looking back, I may say that this is now a new book, adjusted to the new facts of the last two years. I must confess that I'm pleased with the final result, and, if I may say so, a better book than the original one.

I must recognize the effort of my personal assistant, Roseli Mayan, in typing and reviewing it.

My son, João Mauricio Teixeira da Costa, with his Yale master's degree made the final revision of my high school English.

I hope you enjoy this effort.

Also, I do not wish to forget the contributions to the original work in Portuguese: Patricia Tambourgi, who helped me to conclude the book, and Edison de Freitas for reviewing it.

My last thanks go to Ambassador Marcos Azambuja, and to Merval Pereira of the Academia Brasileira de Letras, who contributed to the Portuguese version.

Fundação Dom Cabral for their contribution regarding Brazilian Corporations, also updated.

Finally, my thanks to the personnel of Anthem Press for their patience and collaboration to improve this book.

FOREWORD

Even our closest neighbors are distant. I don't start with this apparent paradox to seek some rhetorical effect, but because it seems essential to understand the historical, geographical and, finally, political and economic circumstances of Brazil's international insertion.

Take South America. The region has almost always, over the centuries, been a strategic backwater. We see the signs of this long stability in borders that remain in the same place, in a narrative with few traumatic ruptures, in the absence of major military conflicts among the regional condominiums and in the virtual inexistence of our problems on the list of those issues that occupy the international agenda first and foremost.

As meager compensation for our delay in following—and even seeking to influence—the events and trends that affected, first and most profoundly, other more central or less peripheral regions of the world, we gained additional time for reflection and, to some extent, could learn from the experiences of others, especially in times of pandemic.

With the extraordinary acceleration of science and technology in recent years and the irresistible impact of the current cycle of globalization, this lag has become even more costly and dysfunctional. I can find no consoling compensation for it now, and I even believe that, if it persists, our ability to compete and advance will perhaps be seriously impaired.

With Covid-19, the world economy and our circumstances have, because of the pandemic, suffered profound repercussions that will extend (and may even intensify) for the foreseeable future and will continue to define the economic and sociopolitical framework in which we will all have to operate and survive.

Roberto Teixeira da Costa knows this as well as anyone and he has been around this vast world collecting experiences and watching the line move. And, each time he returns to Brazil, he brings the news that it is imperative that we seek an agile and competitive insertion in this new international order which, without our knowledge—and, if we are not careful, to our disadvantage—is rapidly consolidating.

Brazil, as always, vast and ever more numerous, is sailing with the current, but without decisively changing the level of its insertion in the world. For a few years, it managed to create the hope (I would almost say the conviction) that its time had come, and that it would finally fulfill the great destiny that was waiting for it, always a little further down the road. Years of relative discouragement follow, and the great national ambitions are, once again, simply postponed.

We are watching the world transform itself and even more accelerate its transformation processes, and Brazil runs the risk of losing the space it could naturally aspire to in the future and still uncertain world order in face of the changes brought about by Covid-19.

We already have the fourth industrial revolution underway in the world, and we haven't even completed the homework of the third. In the universe of intelligence—now also increasingly artificial—we still measure our weight with old scales.

Roberto Teixeira da Costa's research that informs this book is the result of mature and always up-to-date reflection and of frequent contacts, in several countries, with public and private actors who promote the changes in expectations and in the rules of the game that we face today. What is new is the sense of urgency that Roberto lends to his reflections. With the pandemic, this urgent invitation to reflection and action that Roberto makes in his book gains more relevance and actuality.

What causes despair in Brazil is, above all, the gap between perception of the illness and therapeutic action.

For Covid-19, vaccines are being tested and applied. And for Brazil? In this case, we know how to diagnose the patient. Only so far we have not been able to treat it with speed and with the best procedures. The message is clear: we have to move faster and make fewer mistakes. The price of our delay may be growing irrelevance. A ray of hope appeared in mid-December, when four vaccines were positively tested and approved in some countries around the world.

Marcos Azambuja[1]

---

1 Marcos Azambuja, from Rio de Janeiro, is a career diplomat with a long professional career: he was Brazil's Ambassador to France (1997–2003) and Argentina (1992–97), Itamaraty's secretary-general (1990–92), coordinator of the Rio-92 Conference and head of the Brazilian Delegation for Disarmament and Human Rights Affairs, in Geneva (1989–90).

PRESENTATION

The original version of my book in Portuguese was written before the out-break of the Covid-19 pandemic and the war in Ukraine.

Fear was everybody's minds as we waited to see how the world would react to that destruction of values, and what would be the role of the public and private sectors.

Our main focus was on how Brazil would react, the consequences for our economy and the impact on society. The fear was no longer exclusively for Brazil but also for the world, generating great insecurity. Another reason for this uneasiness was the election of Donald Trump in the United States, later succeeded by Joe Biden, and the consequences for globalization and multilateralism. At that point we had to look back and see, based on our experience in international affairs, how to face the new challenges for the future and not forget the main issue. Isolation?

"Nothing makes Brazilians happier than isolation" were the words said by former president Fernando Henrique Cardoso in his institute on 2 April 2020. This was in line with my personal experience and the purpose of this book. In over forty years dedicated to international relations in different institutions associated with world affairs, our detachment from the foreign engagement of our country was made clear.

Thus, I felt the need to delve deeper into that and investigate the reasons for this behavior after many interviews about why Brazilians do not dedicate themselves to foreign relations.

Through that learning and thinking I perceived a distance, or even in particular situations, a complete alienation from any themes related to foreign policy by our business community and other elites engaged.

In different circumstances it was quite evident the lack of interest in discussing what was happening elsewhere in the world and what would be the implications for our country.

That distance was the reason that led me to embark in the project of writing this book. In the process my intention was to look for reasons to contradict the original thesis of the book—"Why is Brazil afraid of the world?" I found no formal disagreements, but mainly different explanations to justify this position. That was long before the Covid-19 outbreak, the pandemic and its consequences.

Thus, the main purpose for writing the book remains valid. Hopefully, the perspective of Lula's return as head of state will bring Brazil back to the international scene, which most countries of the north and south are looking for.

Part 1

DIAGNOSTICS

Chapter 1

THE SICK WORLD: THE COVID-19 PANDEMIC AND ITS IMPACT

The year 2020 is unprecedented in human history. It is a watershed. The feeling is that we are adrift, not knowing whether the storm is over or whether the worst is yet to come. And the bonanza still seems to be far away. We have entered a war against an invisible enemy!

In the middle of the second half of 2019, China was beginning to report the first cases of the new disease, without world politicians paying attention to the catastrophic possibilities that that "little flu" could cause worldwide.

"Gripezinha" was the term used by current Brazilian president Jair Bolsonaro to refer to Covid-19, the name of the disease, according to the World Health Organization (WHO). By 5 April 2021, WHO had already recorded 130,422,190 confirmed cases and 2,842,135 deaths. In Brazil, by the same date, 12,910,082 cases had been confirmed, with 328,206 deaths.[1]

Our president, who in July 2020 also tested positive for Covid-19, was not alone in underestimating the effects of the pandemic. The United States, India and Mexico also delayed adopting radical measures of social isolation and paid a high price, becoming the countries most affected by the disease. As President Trump ran for reelection, the United States led the world at that time in number of cases of Covid-19, reaching 300,000 deaths, a number greater than the losses of American soldiers in World War II.

And something that would seem impossible to happen, or even just figments of the imagination of science fiction authors, has become reality: the pandemic made the capitalist mode of production suffer the biggest hit in its history on a global level! Previous crises, such as the New York Stock Exchange crash in 1929 or the financial crisis in 2008, bear no resemblance to this complete break brought about by the pandemic. In 2020, the economy almost stopped. Businesses closed. Flights canceled. Tourism and aviation systems in crisis.

---

1 WHO. Available at: https://COVID19.who.int/. Accessed on: 16 Dec. 2021.

One example: the losses of Warren Buffett's investment manager Berkshire Hathaway. He noted, "In the global financial crisis of 2008/2009, the 'economy train' went off the rails. In the coronavirus pandemic, the train was taken off the tracks and put on its side."[2]

By the mid-2020s, the tracks were already beginning to be rebuilt in the case of China, at least. The country, first to face the crisis worldwide, showed signs of recovery, having controlled the pandemic within its borders. Strict quarantine measures imposed on the population had worked, and the country was now breathing less contaminated and economically more stimulating air. The "social isolation" was imposed with an iron fist and with the solidary behavior of its population. Capital markets reacted, and the stock exchanges showed positive behavior. Some of the main stock exchanges, especially in the United States, showed a strong reaction in October. Was the worst over?

What will the trails be post-pandemic? Or will the tracks be obsolete when the pandemic is under control? Are profound changes and transformations still on the way?

From everything from the beginning of the pandemic to the appearance of different vaccines, we have been flooded with plenty of material about Covid-19, immunization and consequences. We've seen it all: from renowned infectologists, specialized doctors, "expert" opinions from different backgrounds, quacks, and so on, without considering agents interested in adding to the confusion, some of them looking out for their own interests. This context was a fertile ground for "fake news" to thrive, greatly intensifying doubts that have settled in the affected population.

Looking ahead, it is clear that the countries where scientific intelligence is concentrated will have to redouble their efforts to draw lessons and learnings from Covid-19, standing together to seek common ground when faced with a new pandemic. Therefore, unity will be fundamental, over and above corporate interests and ideologies.

The Braudel Papers—n. 52, 2022 was a special edition dedicated to "Pandemics and the World Economy,"[3] and among its important insights we must highlight:

> Never in the history of the world has a pandemic so suddenly provoked a global economic upheaval. The coronavirus pandemic (Covid-19) impacts billions of people on all continents, with a stream of surprises

---

2 *O Estado de S. Paulo.* Available at: http://bit.ly/2Zouwca.

3 Available at: *https://www.braudel.com/wp-content/uploads/2022/12/Pandemias-e-Economia-mundial-53_en.pdf.*

that the world struggles to understand. They now have fed into pending conflicts over the structure of the world economy.

The covid pandemic is the fourth shock to strike at the world economy since the global financial crisis of 2008. This shock was the culmination of trends that simultaneously produced an acceleration of financial activity, the expanding role of China in world trade and a new scale and diversity of digital activity.

There is no known way that complex societies could have prepared in advance for adversities of this magnitude, even though emergency provisions have been fortified in recent decades. Unforeseen crises appear, as in today's conflict between Russia and Ukraine, leading to the worse price and supply shock in commodities since the Arab-Israeli war of 1973, with the worse disruption of wheat supplies since the outbreak of the First World War in 1914.

New York and São Paulo show striking affinities. Both are giant cities that grew with migration, attracting talented and ambitious people from the rest of the world. Both now are regional concentrations of the coronavirus pandemic that burst the boundaries of knowledge and control. Doctors, nurses and support staff faced similar challenges at Elmhurst Hospital in the New York borough of Queens, in a poor neighborhood packed with immigrants of varied origins, and at São Paulo's Hospital das Clinicas, a huge public institution that is the ultimate port of call for the desperate. Patients and families demanded tests for coronavirus, not yet available.

The impact in Amazonia is vast, a dynamic region, impacted by waves of migration and new technologies attacking its rich resource base, with new cities rising amid the world's biggest rainforest, now threatened and receding, with multiplying patches of forest stripped for cattle-raising, crops, and wildcat gold mining, ever more mechanized for digging deeper. They are opposed by a growing number of Brazilians and foreigners alarmed by prospects of destruction of the world's largest tropical forest.

The population of Manaus surged during Amazonia's rubber boom of the late 19th Century, from 39,000 in 1890 to 76,000 in 1920, then doubling again and again, to 140,000 in 1950, to 314,000 in 1970. By that time military rulers had created a subsidized duty-free zone in Manaus to protect Amazonia from foreign incursion, allowing foreign investors to import and assemble duty-free parts for many products – transistor radios, cellphones, TVs, computers and motorcycles—for export to the rest of Brazil. A busy international airport landed factory parts as well as tourists who explored the river system. By 1980 the population of Manaus doubled again to 642,000, then doubled again to 1.4 million by 2000, approaching 3 million today in an expanded metropolitan region.

As deaths surged in Manaus by April 2020, cemeteries were so overwhelmed that workers were ordered to bury five corpses in the same grave. So many died that the city cut mass burial grounds out of thick forest. Doctors and nurses, unpaid for several months, fled the city. Many with symptoms of covid chose to stay home, scared of dying alone in hospitals.

The Gold of Our Time

Life is known, to a reasonable degree, but the future of life is unknown. The world economy is shaken by a sudden storm, moving with speed and scale never before seen in times of peace. According to the Bank for International Settlements (BIS), the coordinating agency for the world's central banks:

> The past year has felt like an eternity. It is probably too early to tell, but future economic historians might consider the Covid-19 pandemic a defining moment of the 21st Century. When, just over a decade ago [in 2008], the Great Financial Crisis hit the global economy, it was rightly considered such a moment. The pandemic's legacy could be even deeper and longer-lasting.

At the last quarter of 2022 in some of the largest cities of Brazil, the surge of a new variant of Covid was identified and some of the measures of protection were reestablished.

We do not know whether the pandemic will subside with mass inoculations in privileged and targeted populations, whether herd immunities gained from prior waves of infection by other diseases will protect more people, whether outbreaks will return repeatedly, or whether Covid-19 will remain embedded in populations like other endemic diseases, as a low-level threat to most people but deadly to a few.

What we do know is that the present pandemic accelerated basic changes already evolving in human societies. It impacts political priorities, costs, economic security of populations, natural resource limitations, the organization of business and work, the structure of world trade and opportunities of young people for education, jobs and creative activity, among many other contingencies. Many complex societies are weakened by rigidities in the sharing of wealth that must be renegotiated. In contending with these difficulties, and facing stringencies in public finances, governments face hard choices between repressed consumption and chronic inflation.

The parameters of organized economic life are shifting. The boundaries of elasticity become narrower, even as political institutions contend with broader and heavier demands. The Russian invasion of Ukraine clarifies these choices, as political institutions worldwide seek to control the covid pandemic. The goal for most is stability of democratic institutions, opposed by servants of authoritarian rule. There is no middle ground.

"The Russian invasion of Ukraine has put an end to the globalization we have experienced over the last three decades," warned Larry Fink, head of the giant investment bank BlackRock, predicting a shrinkage in overseas investments that will reduce the reach of supply chains and inflate costs. Inflation becomes, once again, a major issue in the United States, with consumer prices rising in the fastest surge in four decades. With the central bank paralyzed by political demands and controversy, successive surges of emergency spending in the pandemic totaled 25% of GDP, the highest on record in peacetime, helping to drive a new wave of global economic expansion. This drive reached a climax with U.S. intervention, with money and weapons, on the side of democratic forces in Ukraine resisting a Russian invasion.

Cooperation is one of the mysteries of evolution. Despite shocking episodes of disease and warfare, humanity has repeatedly reorganized and improved the quality of life. Epidemics of the past, costly in lives and suffering, nevertheless yielded new standards of civilization. The Black Death of bubonic plague in early modern Europe led to the invention of quarantine practices, a new price for labor, redistribution of land tenure and cultural developments such as expanded literacy and the invention of printing. The cholera epidemics of the 19th Century drove new public health practices and better physical and social infrastructure.

The economic and public health crises of the past, when overcome, inspired new thinking and new priorities. The expansion of the world economy, measured in centuries or decades, has paused for now, posing new challenges. We need consolidation, as humanely as possible. These challenges demand new levels of human cooperation, involving more productive public investment, more just taxation, better education, more opportunities for young people and reduction of privileges. It will be hard to escape the choices posed by this need for cooperation.

Chapter 2

HYPOTHESES ABOUT BRAZIL'S ISOLATION ON THE INTERNATIONAL SCENE

If you know the enemy and know yourself, you need not fear the result of a hundred battles. If you know yourself, but not the enemy, for every victory gained you will also suffer a defeat. If you know neither the enemy nor yourself, you will succumb in every battle.

—Sun Tzu, *The Art of War*

In these pandemic-ridden times, social isolation, physical distancing and the creation of survival protocols have become essential parts of our daily life. Techniques to keep some distance from other people have been fundamental to lessen the impact of the novel coronavirus on world populations.

Historically the international insertion of Brazil has always been characterized by isolation and distancing from other world states. Eventual rapprochements with certain states—such as the Bolsonaro administration's blind march toward Donald Trump's America—have been episodic and selective. In terms of its international insertion, Brazil has for a long time sought isolation and only approached those nations regarded as family or where a specific commercial interest was present.

It would be an interesting exercise to try and unveil the factors that have led Brazil to this isolationist attitude. More than an intellectual exercise, however, we should try to understand these variables, in order to identify the sore points that effectively must be considered to advance Brazil's international standing.

No matter how much I've reflected on this theme and discussed it with journalists, colleagues and specialists, the compass of our problems always points to scenarios of inadequacies and excesses in our social organization. It seems to me that shortfalls inherent to each of them have contributed significantly to our current situation.

Beyond the huge size of the country itself, one must consider the comfort zone our domestic market provides for Brazilian corporations. A market composed of Portuguese-speaking consumers, overwhelmingly Brazilian, whose cultural and regional preferences are easy to understand, where the rules are written in Portuguese, in a respectably sized territory. Domestic conveniences are irresistible in comparison with the possibility of seeking external markets where the challenges and risks are greater and more diverse, such as the difficulties of adaptation to different regulatory regimes, the lack of financial resources and teams without international experience.

The domestic market is not only the privileged arena for action but also the sacred area for protectionism. After all, when one talks of the internal or domestic market, tariff protection has been the main configuration for Brazil historically. It is not by accident that we score so low in economic freedom and competitiveness indicators, as well as in share of international trade flows. Again, we must repeat: Brazil is one of the world's countries least open to international trade. And domestic market protection has become a key factor in business policy, strategic planning and lobbying efforts.

Up to this point one would think that the Brazilian business community chose not to gamble beyond national borders. But it is also necessary to point a finger at a government that imposes complex bureaucratic norms on those who want to internationalize, discouraging them from going abroad.

It is true that the so-called whale countries such as the United States, Russia and China currently privilege their domestic markets. Trump's nationalistic "America First" policies as well as his (and Biden's) trade disputes are examples. Our preference for the domestic market, therefore, cannot carry all the blame for our limited international presence. Other elements must be remembered to compose a more complete picture of the situation. Elements that restrict expansion overseas such as the protectionist policies of other countries, which may restrict international trade.

Scarcity

The land that is so fertile that "everything that is planted, grows" is also a land of scarcity. Multiple kinds of scarcity. The shortages in government, corporations and human resources dictate the speed of internationalization in Brazil—or rather, the lack of it.

What follows is a list of examples of bottlenecks that hold Brazil back from a stronger, more assured course in the world:

1. A disregard for long-term planning in foreign policy in our domestic political debates. Given the magnitude of our internal problems, foreign

policy has never been a major preoccupation for most Brazilians, being often relegated to an intellectual elite revolving around the career foreign service bureaucracy (the "Itamaraty");

2. The lack of a culture of exports of high value-added products. Historically and anthropologically, we are heirs of colonialism, living from exports of primary products. The country was "bought," not "sold," meaning that importers (frequently British) and their agents would come to Brazil looking for commodities of interest to them. We nurtured, therefore, a degree of self-indulgence, making available what we had instead of taking to the world as traders and merchants;

3. Brazil was born as a centralizing state. Domestic corporations have always been highly dependent on government;

4. Dependency also, of Brazilian corporations who want to internationalize, on the Itamaraty. There is a lack of direct articulation of the business community with partners abroad. The Ministry of Foreign Affairs has always been very diligent in occupying spaces here and abroad, and it is easier for businesspeople to talk to Brasília rather than to Washington, London or Frankfurt. The result has been an excessive dependency on the ministry and its representatives abroad. More recently we have seen some of our embassies and consulates-general better prepared to offer assistance to businesses;

5. There are no public policies backing the internationalization of the business sector and supporting companies that wish to invest abroad. In fact, there is an immense amount of red tape and tax questions that make international expansion harder or, at the very least, don't make it any easier. Depending on the administration in office there may be more or less attention paid to foreign policy. A strong dependency on the state is a heritage that, as we've seen, comes from colonial times. Under president Bolsonaro there have been many promises of change in this pattern of behavior, but practical results have not been felt. It should be noted that the current international situation has not been helpful, on the contrary, more isolation.

6. Human resources deficiencies. There are many leaders who are simply not capable of engaging in a dialogue with their international counterparts. Brazilians do travel frequently abroad, but mostly for tourism and culture. I have participated in some trips organized by trade organizations and their participants frequently dispersed after registering their presence in the opening session of the event. As a rule, they were not prepared to engage with their peers from around the world. And we do not prepare adequately for debates on a level playing field with people from abroad,

as I have discussed in my previous book, *Nem só de marketing*, co-written with Susanna Sancovsky.[1] On the positive side, however, the demand for courses in international relations in Brazilian universities has been increasing sharply in recent years, which is a positive sign;

7. Modest and often irrelevant participation in international meetings. It is hard to mobilize corporations for these events. Our participation in the World Economic Forum in Davos, for example, is not in proportion with our size and importance. By contrast, the number of participants from countries such as China and India, and even Argentina and Mexico, is striking;

8. The Foreign Relations Commissions of the Chamber of Deputies and Senate are not relevant and do not define positions in Brazilian foreign policy. The discussions mostly do not leave the walls of the parliament buildings and rarely contribute to the wider debate about Brazil and the rest of the world.

In the interesting and still relevant journal article "Política externa: privilégio do Poder Executivo"[2] Vera de Araújo Grillo discusses the minimal role of the Brazilian congress in relation to foreign policy, both in terms of setting objectives as well as in their execution.

It is worth nothing that when the article was written there seemed to be a growing consciousness of the power possessed by Congress. On the other hand, it was still necessary to establish channels of information, technical as well as political, formal as well as informal, with members of Congress!

According to the author, the main actors who played important roles on the political and institutional stage were the president, the minister of foreign relations and the National Security Council, all within the executive branch.

It is striking that in the period from 1964 to 1986 the guidelines of foreign policy were established and labeled in accordance with the personal "style" of the president of the republic, therefore associated with the head of the executive. Castelo Branco's "automatic alignment," Médici's "diplomacy of prosperity," Geisel's "responsible pragmatism," Figueiredo's "ecumenism" are cited, as well as Sarney's "diplomacy for results."

We did not, therefore, have a state foreign policy. We had the different policies of each administration.

---

1 Editora Conex, São Paulo, 2005.
2 In *Política e Estratégia*, v. IV, n. 1 (Jan–Mar 1986).

It is evident that, whatever the period and the president, Congress seemed to be absent from this aspect of our political life, except for the items of the strictest constitutional competence.

Grillo reminds us that the so-called New Republic did not innovate in this field, following the steps of the previous regime both in the policy-setting mechanisms (National Security Council, Foreign Ministry, military ministers) and in the maintenance of the same type of performance—as in the case of foreign debt negotiations, in which the Foreign Ministry did not have much of a role and Congress even less so.

Of the presidents that followed José Sarney—Fernando Collor, Itamar Franco, Fernando Henrique Cardoso, Luiz Inácio Lula da Silva, Dilma Rousseff, Michel Temer and now Jair Bolsonaro—FHC and Lula were particularly active abroad. Michel Temer, though only an interim president, also sought to leave his mark in international affairs. The pattern noted by Araújo Grillo remains in place—our Congress seems to be afraid of the world!

9. Lack of a well-articulated subnational diplomacy, similar to that of countries such as Canada, for example. In broad strokes, subnational diplomacy happens when entities other than the federal government, such as states and cities, contact foreign entities directly to solve their problems without interference from federal diplomacy. This picture may be beginning to change. Under Governor João Dória the state of São Paulo, going against this perception, has been very active. In the case of medical equipment to combat the Covid-19 pandemic many states were forced to procure it directly, without any help from Brasília. In COP 27, the state of Amazon took a leading and independent role in the meeting, associated with other countries of the region;

10. Lack of fluency in foreign languages. Our capacity to communicate in foreign languages is rather limited. Most politicians only speak Portuguese, and up to the 1970s–80s foreign languages were practically exclusive to career diplomats. In the corporate world as well, foreign language proficiency was never important, except perhaps in financial markets, where knowledge of English is practically a requirement. Today institutions such as Fundação Getúlio Vargas offer college-level degrees with integral instruction in English.

The Chinese, who not too long ago were barely able to express themselves in English, now have total control of the language. The change has been dramatic. In my time at Columbia University, and also at other leading

American and European institutions of higher learning, I was struck by the substantial presence of Chinese students;

11. Lack of awareness among our elites of the relevant role played by Brazil in the world. We stay focused on the short term and keep trying to solve problems from the past. I am struck by how often, not only in the business world but also in other segments of so-called "elite" society, such as business associations, museums, schools, corporate boards, themes from the past (never quite solved or disentangled) take up the lion's share of our attention.

It should also be noted that Brazil has the sixth worst elite in the world, according to the ranking published by the Foundation for Value Creation in Switzerland.[3] A low ranking indicates an elite group that extracts more value than it creates. "The Brazilian elite is in the rent-seeking category. Our worst rankings are in the state rent-extraction category, rent-seeking by producers, and labor rent-seeking."[4]

12. The press, in general, does not provide adequate coverage of international aspects and issues in their news reporting. A case in point has been the discontinuing of *Política Externa*, the quarterly created in 1992 by publisher Fernando Gasparian. After two decades of uninterrupted publishing, it was discontinued, despite the efforts of Helena Gasparian.

With an enormous collection of articles of the highest quality and counting on an Editorial Board with names such as Fernando Henrique Cardoso, Hélio Jaguaribe, Celso Lafer, Marcos Azambuja, Rubens Ricupero, Carlos Eduardo Lins da Silva (including myself!), the journal could not find enough adverting support, be it in print or on the internet. It also used to be distributed to all Brazilian embassies. It certainly left a void. We hope it will eventually come back, in print or on-line. Recently CEBRI has tried to fill the void by launching the journal *Política Externa* (Issue No. 3 July–September 2022) with articles of experts on foreign policy topics.

Excesses

The imbalance also manifests itself through excesses:

---

3 https://elitequality.org.
4 Fernando Nery, "Piores elites do Mundo," *O Estado de S. Paulo*, 8 December, 2020.

1. Corporatism, including by industry associations, which tend to be highly protectionist. Once again, another example of the "invisible hand" of the heavy heritage of our political and economic history;
2. So-called Custo Brasil, or Brazil Cost, a crucial factor:
   a. Excessive bureaucracy;
   b. High and complicated taxes;
   c. Labor-related costs too high when compared to many developed countries;
   d. High social security costs;
   e. Frequent alterations in regulations, affecting predictability;
   f. Excessive legislation, incompatible with Brazil's international competitiveness;
   g. Conflicts between federal, state and local governments.

Regarding "Custo Brasil," *Folha de São Paulo* newspaper published in its 21 July 2019 edition a special section with the headline "Custo Brasil reaches R$1.5 trillion and makes businesses less competitive." On average, companies from OECD countries spend 38 percent less on taxes than Brazilian ones. Brazilian corporations must work 89 percent more than the OECD average in terms of man-hours to prepare tax statements. Inefficient logistics cost twice as much as the OECD average. Electric energy is also more expensive but new renewable sources such as solar and wind will provide more competition.

A research paper by Deloitte found that Brazilian corporations with annual sales of more than R$ 7 billion/year spend 34,000 man-hours per year with tax-related bureaucracy.[5] Simplification of the tax code is a perennial demand in all tax reform discussions.

3. Timidity. Do we realize the importance of our country in the international scene? Is it still a reality that we are dominated by a "stray dog complex," as immortalized by playwright Nelson Rodrigues?
4. Passivity. We do not take the initiative. In most cases we are just followers. As the popular saying goes, "If you don't raise dust, you eat dust."

Will the novel coronavirus compel us to seek a new approach in our international coexistence, in issues such as navigating the growing U.S.–China rivalry or our insertion in international trade flows?

---

5 *Valor Econômico* newspaper, downloaded from https://glo.bo/3u3MRt1.

A new international political geography, certainly more complex than the one we've had in the recent past, will force us to position to defend our interests in a way we have not done before.

It seems that the consequences of the Covid-19 pandemic and the war in Ukraine will force us to face a new reality and its impact on our society. Maybe this may be the opportunity to redirect our actions toward a better path to economic and social development.

In any case, this crisis, like any other, harbors opportunities. We must make a big effort to seek unity to conquer this crisis and leave it in better shape than we entered it.

Part 2

WHY HAVE FEAR?

The only thing that we have to fear is fear itself.
—Franklin Delano Roosevelt, in the 1922 campaign
for the presidency of the United States

Chapter 3

INTERNATIONALIZATION OF BRAZILIAN CORPORATIONS

World, world, vast world,
if my name were Raymond
it would be a rhyme, not a solution.
World vast world,
wider is my heart.

—Stanza from the "Seven Faces," poem by Carlos
Drummond de Andrade

In this famous verse, Carlos Drummond de Andrade, a well-known Brazilian poet, already recognized, decades ago, the breadth of our globe. Although he also poetically focused on the vastness of his heart, what interests us here is the depth of our country's pockets. And this size depends, in good part, on our capacity for international insertion.

Internationalization is necessary. There is plenty of literature in the world that explains the benefits of a market being exposed to the "wide world." Greater access to consumer markets, production scale gains, among others.

In a survey conducted by our Brazilian Export and Investment Promotion Agency (Apex-Brasil) in 2017, 229 domestic corporations were surveyed. Most of them listed as a motivation for crossing borders the possibility of increasing sales (72.7 percent), as well as to diversify risks (65.3 percent) and to protect themselves from local market instabilities (61.3 percent).[1] In August 2020, Apex-Brasil launched a training program for exports in Amazonas and Roraima.

A PhD from Brunel University, a specialist on the subject and a woman who moves through a mostly male environment, Betania Tanure points out other reasons for going international: growth, conquering other markets, obtaining economies of scale, strengthening the competitive position,

---

1 Available at: https://bit.ly/3prgbpZ.

increasing profitability, reducing the risk of operating in a single market and accessing capital markets in other countries. And I would add, gaining experience in technological management and artificial intelligence (AI). Although she points out the risks, uncertainties and complexities associated with the internationalization process, she explains that when the path is well followed, the cost–benefit ratio tends to be positive.

In recent decades, global economic openness has been unprecedented. Thanks largely to the World Trade Organization (WTO), and its predecessor, the General Agreement on Tariffs and Trade, trade barriers have been significantly reduced. From the Uruguay Round alone (1986–94) forward, developed countries have cut tariffs on industrial goods by 40 percent, averaging around 6.4 percent, according to the WTO.[2] In addition, the number of industrial products free of import duties in these same countries rose from 20 to 44 percent, according to the organization's data.[3]

World trade has been going through some tough times, pulled by the back and forth of the Trade War between China and the United States. After seeing an auspicious 2017, with a 4.7 percent increase in the volume of trade in goods, the highest growth among the previous six years, and with member exports totaling US$17.43 trillion, international trade has slowed down again since 2018. If the forecasts for 2019 were already even more modest, 2020 appears as a major negative milestone in the world economy.

As it reaches 25 years of existence in 2020, the WTO probably faces its greatest challenge since its creation. The United States, during the Trump administration, antagonized the WTO up to a point of almost paralyzing their activities.

Covid-19 led the organization to create a web page dedicated exclusively to the impacts of the new scenario in international trade: for the WTO, the pandemic is an unprecedented disruption, in which production and consumption have retreated drastically. According to Roberto Azevêdo, director-general of the entity until mid-2020, "the numbers are ugly," with a forecast of a significant drop in trade in goods compared to 2019, in a scenario worse than the 2008–9 financial crisis.[4]

To mitigate the paralysis of the WTO, a new structure was created by a group of countries, composed by three judges (one of them was the Brazilian ambassador Graça Lima), the so-called Interim Group of arbitration and

---

2 WTO. *The WTO at 25: A Message from the Director-General*. Available at: http://bit.ly /2NuEW7d. Accessed on: 28 Jan. 2020.
3 Available at: http://bit.ly/37k2xOS. Accessed on: 30 Aug. 2019.
4 Available at: http://bit.ly/2N5lo9Q.

appeal. It is a plurilateral body created on a temporary basis, due to the fact that the WTO Body of Appeal was not functioning.

Before the pandemic hit earlier this year, the organization stressed the importance of global value chains as dominant in international trade:

> The predictable market conditions fostered by the WTO have combined with improved communications to enable the rise of global value chains. Confident in their ability to move components and associated services across multiple locations, businesses have been able to disaggregate manufacturing production across countries and regions. Trade within these value chains today accounts for almost 70% of total merchandise trade.[5]

And it is precisely the value chains, especially the more complex ones, that have been most impacted by the Covid-19 pandemic, and, they will certainly be rethought.

According to the WTO, one of the positive effects of value chains (pre-pandemic) was the impact on developing countries, with opportunities to integrate into the global economy and generate more jobs and income.[6] However, the division of the participation in world trade activities remained, until then, highly concentrated: 52 percent of total international trade in goods was carried out by the top 10 traders, with the three largest of them— China, the United States and Germany—controlling one-third of world trade. With regard to services, the concentration scenario is even more pronounced: developing countries accounted for only 34 percent of the total.[7] In a post-pandemic scenario, we may see, in the short term, greater diversification in supply chains. And developing countries may lose relative space.

At a meeting of the Group of 20 (virtual) held in October 2020, President Bolsonaro advocated a reform of the WTO. At that meeting, the president defined the WTO as a "key element" for the recovery of the global economy. He advocated progress on three pillars: (i) negotiations, (ii) dispute settlement and (iii) monitoring and transparency. Brazil has the ambition to reduce agricultural subsidies with the same goodwill with which some countries seek

---

5 WTO. *The WTO at 25: A Message from the Director-General.* Available at: https://bit.ly /2NuEW7d. Accessed on: 28 Jan. 2020.
6 WTO. *Technological Innovation, Supply Chain Trade, and Workers in a Globalized World: Global Value Chain Development Report 2019.* Available at: https://bit.ly/3pmeLNb. Accessed on: 28 Jan. 2020.
7 Each year, the WTO publishes a report with comments and data on the previous period and projections and trends for world trade.

promotion and trade of industrial goods. The WTO must contemplate the stimulation of investments and the creation of fair and fruitful conditions for international trade, not only in goods but also in services.

G20 is short for "Group of 20." It was formed by the finance ministers and central bank chiefs of the 19 largest economies in the world and the European Union. Created in 1999, after crises on the world stage in the 1990s, it seeks to favor international negotiation, integrating and creating an expanded dialogue of countries that together represent 90 percent of the world economy, 80 percent of world trade (including intra-European Union trade) and two-thirds of the world population. It analyzes and promotes discussion between richer and emerging countries about different policies related to the promotion of international financial stability and addresses issues that are beyond the responsibilities of individual member countries.

In their most recent meeting of November 2022 in Bali, the focus was on the war in Ukraine and the efforts to reach peace.

It emerged amid pressure from different countries that were part of the so-called G8 (the group of the seven most industrialized economies plus Russia, the rich countries) and, effectively after the Washington meeting in 2009, decided that the G20 would be the new permanent international council for economic cooperation. The topics discussed at the regular meetings are not limited exclusively to economic issues. At the October 2020 meeting, of course, the topic of Covid-19 was central.

Where Is Brazil in International Trade?

According to *the Foreign Trade Department of the Economics Ministry*, in 2022:[8]

- Brazilian foreign trade from January to October 2022 already reached US$ 510 billion, surpassing the total of US$ 500 billion in 2021.
- Exports for the month of October reached US$ 28 billion, also a historical record and 19.1 percent above the same period of the previous year.
- Exports increased to all regions of the world, with Asia as our biggest market followed by Europe, United States and South America.

Our trade balance has remained, in recent years, positive. Even in 2022, a surplus of US$ 55 billion is estimated. Again, a caveat is required about the consequences of the pandemic on international trade. The recovery from the

---

8 See https://balanca.economia.gov.br/balanca/pg_principal_bc/principais_resulta-dos.html.

pandemic will be one of the most relevant factors in the projections for the resumption of international trade.

This behavior can be explained mainly by two factors. On the export side, our strong presence in commodity exports, (i) China appearing as our first market and (ii) the fact that our low economic growth did not cause imports to increase. In 2019, we had a deterioration in exports (falling soybean sales) and some increase in imports.

In the world of foreign direct investment (FDI), it is true that we have increased our presence as a protagonist in some developed countries, due to favorable factors (foreign market and exchange rate). In more recent years, however, the low growth and the crisis that many of our companies have experienced have caused businessmen to put the brakes on expanding abroad, including some divestments.

A leading Brazilian foreign trade journal[9] published the article "The industry's international agenda 2020—a roadmap for a competitive international insertion," very much in line with our concerns. The text is by Carlos Eduardo Abijaodi, director of CNI, the main organization representing the Brazilian industrial sector. The document, prepared for the fifth consecutive year, presents actions distributed along four axes: (a) defense of interests in trade policy, (b) services to support the internationalization of companies, (c) actions in strategic markets and (d) international cooperation. The internationalization support services include: (a) governance for services, (b) regulation of services and (c) supply of services.[10] It is quite positive that the most representative body of industry is making these services available to its member federations. The article ends by stating that the demand for a national foreign trade strategy precedes the Covid-19 pandemic, which becomes even more relevant and pertinent every day. Also, the war in Ukraine will affect world politics and trade flows.

But the fact is that Brazil remains closed. In the international economic freedom ranking, in which the economies of 180 countries are analyzed, Brazil appears in position number 144, classified as a mostly closed country.[11] Recluse and afraid of the world. When searching for dissonant thoughts, I only found echoes to my perception. I had no disagreements, but rather, explanations of the different hypotheses.

---

9 *Funcex Magazine*, no. 143, p. 24, Apr.–Jun. 2010.
10 Available at: https://bit.ly/3diSeOV.
11 The Index of Economic Freedom is compiled by the Heritage Foundation in partnership with the *Wall Street Journal*. Available at: https://www.heritage.org/index/.

The war in Ukraine, with all its consequences—sanctions against Russia as well as the Russian reaction, reducing the supply and increasing the cost of gas, oil and fertilizers to the Western world—had a strong impact in international trade and, consequently, in growth. Data by the end of October 2022, with high inflation, and higher interest rates, point to a global deceleration.

The question that economists haven't answered is: Will the United States and China face an economic deceleration or a recession?

S&P Global releases a composite activity index that includes services and manufactures for the United States that dropped to 49.5 points in September and 47.3 on October, the lowest number since 2009. Numbers below 50 indicate a contraction, which seems to be happening in the last quarter of the year.

Internationalization of Brazilian Small Business[12]

Globalization, particularly for small corporations, is a process that redefines and expands forms of articulation and performance of national economies and strategies, promoting companies to access international markets. The involvement of small and medium-sized enterprises (SMEs) remains less expressive when compared with the participation of large companies, but in recent years has been gradually changing.

Surviving in a competitive and dynamic market is a challenge to an organization of any size. It requires a participation in an external market and expands the forms of articulation and performance of national economies and encourages companies to access the international market, but still, SMEs were less involved in the global market than large companies. Globally, SMEs represent the backbone of any country's economy. Hence, public support should play an important role in promoting greater internationalization and should focus on the main barriers to SMEs' internationalization.

The expansion of companies has evolved from traditional exports to remote clients or the opening of overseas branches, to international presence through commercial or strategic partnerships with local and foreign companies. The process of globalization has, furthermore, progressed from the formation of multinational companies to the internationalization of their own productive chains through cooperation between independent companies that operate in different countries. This process has helped to increase the competitiveness of small businesses and provide them with access to new markets previously dominated by large corporations.

---

12   This section is based on a paper prepared by King's College scholar Darcio Pimenta.

Internationalization should be viewed as a key to increase competitiveness, influencing the development of countries in a global context and facilitating access to new resources and markets and also in management structure. Most of the internationalization process was originated in Europe and the United States. However, lately in China a significant change has been observed in the past decades when emerging economies have become more attractive to business. In fact, there has been a significant increase in the number of small companies from developing economies, including Brazil, particularly funded by access to venture capital sponsored among others by institutional investors.

The Chinese economy is a clear example, by providing more opportunities for the import of goods and services and facilitating the absorption of innovation and the adoption of new technologies from abroad.

In Brazil, the internationalization of companies began in earnest almost a century after it did in European and American companies, where the process started after World War I. The process has taken off, however, over the past few decades, mainly due to favorable economic national and international conditions that have made Brazil the largest economy in Latin America.

Despite growth prospects for Brazilian SMEs, new and old challenges must be overcome, and trade relations became more competitive, especially for small enterprises.

The process of internationalization of Brazilian companies began in the 1970s with foreign investment by some Brazilian companies and banks, looking for their import markets and accessing the capital markets of developed countries. In the 1980s the process continued with large infrastructure companies and some industrial companies moving into external markets.

The period between 1990 and 1994 was marked by a high level of macroeconomic instability and institutional reforms focusing at reducing state interference in the economy. The reforms extended to international integration through trade, financial liberalization and direct foreign investment. This process opened the Brazilian economy to the global market. That initiative focused industrial sectors to competition from foreign products. The main instrument used was the gradual, but significant, reduction of import tariffs from 1990 to 1994. In this period, investments were aimed at operational efficiency, with little fixed investment. The growth of Brazilian entrepreneurs was motivated by the emergence of new business opportunities for small entrepreneurs, both nationally and internationally

In Brazil, and elsewhere, SMEs are engines of job creation. They represent the core of innovation and entrepreneurship. According to a 2018 study from Sebrae—Brazilian Service to support Small Business—small businesses employ more than 50 percent of the labor force. To make this happen, the innovation and the process of management of SMEs may occur in a continuous way to confront the national barriers and the new scenario. The great challenges in adapting to a fast-growing market area: the tax burden effects, the lack of preparation and knowledge of entrepreneurs, among other things, factors that can be decisive for large and small corporations.

Emerging economies, as is the case of the members of Mercosur, often following a gradualist approach to internationalization, first introducing activity in nearby countries (nearby in both geographical and cultural terms), using a conservative strategy for managing the knowledge and learning gained through the process. Because of market saturation some companies decide to go abroad in order to keep growing and to be more competitive.

Entrepreneurs are the driving force of economic growth. In most circumstances, these companies are responsible for launching innovative products and technologies, making the existing ones obsolete and outdated. Thus, the contribution of entrepreneurial economic development occurs by introducing innovation and competition in the local market and is a benefit for the growth of economic activities.

Chapter 4

THE FOURTH INDUSTRIAL REVOLUTION AND THE CHALLENGES FOR INTERNATIONALIZATION

How could a country like Brazil, looking for a higher international presence and more competitiveness in the export sector, add value to its exports, without developing an industrial policy in which technology plays a fundamental role?

The German engineer and economist Klaus Schwab, creator of the *World Economic Forum*, presented, a few years ago, a concept that quickly became the subject of lectures and discussions: the concept of the Fourth Industrial Revolution.

> The technologies of the Fourth Industrial Revolution are truly disruptive—they subvert existing ways of feeling, calculating, organizing, acting, and fulfilling agreements. They represent entirely new ways of creating value for organizations and citizens. They will, over time, transform all the systems that are taken for granted today—from the way we produce and transport goods and services to the way we communicate, collaborate, and enjoy the world around us. In the present, advances in neurotechnology and biotechnology are already forcing us to question what it means to be human.[1]

The world is currently going through a new moment of important transformation catapulted by new technologies and by the interconnection of these technological developments among various fields of knowledge. AI, nanotechnology, biotechnology, robotics and neurotechnology, for example, are combining to transform reality. Even with the seismic movement that

---

1 SCHWAB, K. *Applying the Fourth Industrial Revolution*. São Paulo: Edipro, 2018, pp. 21–22.

affected the markets immediately after the confirmation of the pandemic, what we saw is that high-tech companies kept their value, and some even appreciated substantially.

More than this: the great transformations reverberate through the way human beings relate to each other in the era of the digital revolution, bringing new challenges that can, on one hand, "robotize humanity" or, on the other, "raise humanity to a new collective and moral consciousness."[2]

Countries can either face the current reality that is being forged in such a way as to succumb to transformations that can dismantle economies, or act in such a way as to hitch a ride on the window of opportunity that presents itself. Some see Brazil's backwardness as a chance to burn a few steps. It seems difficult, but not impossible.

Investment in science and technology plays a key role in this regard. If we adopt Schwab's view of the way things are going in the world, we will realize that, in common, the great transformations depend on research and development (R&D) requiring highly refined knowledge in cutting-edge science.

In face of this scenario, the question is: What about Brazil? How is the country dealing with the fourth industrial revolution: As a crisis or as an opportunity?

If we look at the investments in R&D in our country in comparison with the world, we can see that we are a long distance away from the standards required for a developing country. According to UNESCO data, the country's R&D investments represent 1.3 percent of the Gross Domestic Product (with estimates of a drop after the fiscal crisis). "Although short of the more than 4% seen in the leaders and the world average (2%), we invest more in R&D in proportion to GDP than Argentina, Chile, Colombia, and Mexico."[3]

In comparison, if we look at Israel, we will see that the country, perhaps the best placed in the UNESCO ranking, invests 4.2 percent of GDP, with 8,250 researchers per million inhabitants. In Brazil, we have 881 researchers for every million inhabitants.[4] Naturally, Israeli GDP is smaller than that of Brazil, but, proportionally, the degree of prioritization of research in Israel is significantly higher than in Brazil,[5] always remembering that they are two countries with very different territorial dimensions.

---

2 SCHWAB, K. *The Fourth Industrial Revolution*. São Paulo: Edipro, 2016.

3 ALVAREZ, Roberto. Brazil needs a contemporary innovation agenda. Available at: http://glo.bo/2ZuAIiz. Accessed on: 26 Mar. 2019.

4 UNESCO. How much does your country invest in R&D?. Available at: http://bit.ly /3axLwD8. Accessed: 17 Sept. 2019.

5 Ibid.

Innovation leaves much to be desired in Brazil. In a study conducted by researcher Paulo Morceiro, from the Center for Regional and Urban Economics of the University of São Paulo (Nereus–USP), of 37 segments studied, only five approach the technological frontier, with a high level of investment in research. We have low technological density. The biggest investors in R&D in the world, accounting for 80 percent, are the OECD member countries.[6]

In an issue published in the month of September 2019, the journal *Pesquisa* of the São Paulo State Research Support Foundation (FAPESP) dedicated its cover story to the phenomenon of the "scientific diaspora," popularly known as "brain drain." It presents an idea that echoes what has already been discussed throughout this work: that fear of the world that Brazil seems to have. "Brazil historically presents a low degree of mobility of its scientists—a study by sociologist Simon Schwartzman in the 1970s pointed out the tendency to isolation, with few people leaving to study or work, of which many returned," comments Alexandra Ozorio de Almeida, the magazine's editorial director.[7]

In fact, compared to the world, Brazil exchanges few scientists with foreign countries. Based on OECD data, the magazine's report argues that Brazil's international insertion in terms of exports and imports of scientists is "low and stable."

However, the consolidated figures involving skilled workers indicate growth. "Since 2015, when the economy plunged into recession, the number of permanent exits from Brazil is above 20,000 each year. Before that, it had been going up, but it didn't go past 15,000. In 2018, 22,400 people handed in declarations of definitive departure from Brazil." The data are from the IRS obtained through November 2019.[8] If we take the federative states into account, we will see that Roraima is the one that, proportionally, loses the most qualified labor (44 percent), followed by Rio de Janeiro (42 percent) and Rio Grande do Sul (42 percent).[9] Among the most alleged reasons are the unemployment rate, political polarization and crisis, and violence.

Not free from criticism and diverse opinions, another comment often heard that justifies the brain drain is the distance between academia and the private sector. Despite the commitment of some respectable names, the university world has political, and in some cases ideological, restrictions on greater cooperation between the public and private sectors.

---

6 Available at: http://glo.bo/2ZxnkKU. Accessed: 25 Jun. 2019.
7 Almeida, A. O. of "Brains in Motion". FAPESP Research, 2019, p. 7.
8 Available at: http://glo.bo/3s8eGOV. Accessed: 16 Dec. 2019.
9 Available at: http://glo.bo/3qF9q59. Accessed: 23 June 2019.

The largest state research promotion agency in the country, FAPESP adopts a financing policy for both educational and research institutions and for São Paulo companies that seek to develop scientific research, by means of promoting lines specifically designed for private sector undertakings.

In an article published in *Valor*, the executive director of the *Global Federation of Competitiveness Councils*, Roberto Alvarez, PhD in production engineering, describes five points of an innovation agenda for Brazil. Among the points listed, Alvarez comments that the "distant relationship between industry and research is not 'cultural.' It results from legal-institutional barriers, the organization of the public university and its careers, and the lack of effective public-private interface."[10]

Thinking about the benefits gained from exporting and importing in terms of trade is more common. Migrating this thinking into scientific terms is far less usual. At first, it may even seem harmful for scientists to leave the country. The very term "brain drain" presents a negative connotation of the phenomenon. However, the "exportation" of scientists also means the creation of international collaborative networks, which can bring benefits to the object of study, by bringing scientists with different sociocultural and academic backgrounds, which can enrich the study of the research object. "The accumulated knowledge on the subject suggests that if immigration is to experience another professional reality—and not for lack of options—and the country of origin knows how to take advantage of the opportunity, there will be national and individual gains," added the journalist.

One of our interviewees recalled that, unlike Chinese and Indian students, who return to their home country after their studies, particularly in the United States, the same does not happen to many Brazilians. Some of them stated that in different international events, when the number of Brazilian students attending was relevant, many said they would rather stay abroad, where large opportunities are identified to apply their knowledge. Also, they hope for improvements in the political and social situation in Brazil to return home.

Bringing the scientific diaspora debate into the context of the Fourth Industrial Revolution, one perceives a fundamental movement to keep national science abreast of and as part of the most current developments in world science. Encouraging the exchange of domestic science with the most advanced in the world is not a luxury, but rather a necessity and a political strategy to be pursued. Keeping the country close to the frontier of knowledge

---

10 Alvarez, Brazil needs a contemporary innovation agenda.

means trying to reduce and combat the scientific *gap* between developed countries that are leaders in innovation and research, and Brazil.

One possibility that we raise is a greater scientific exchange with Latin America, particularly Argentina, as commented elsewhere in the text. As a defender of the Southern Common Market (Mercosur), I am in favor of its optimization and greater exchanges among its participants. In the specific sector of innovation and scientific knowledge I think that the exchange of information with our neighbors from Buenos Aires would strengthen our ties and allow technological advances. Agreements such as the Southern Common Market (Mercosur) require permanent dialogue and frequent exchanges.

Francis Bacon[11] has never been so current. "Knowing" is still "power." Covid-19 more than ever underscored the importance of technology, and particularly medical science. I believe that preventive medicine will be valued, and the role of technology will be fundamental in this process.

As a result of what we have reflected on here, publicly traded companies that are at the forefront of IT use have had their shares appreciate in value even in the most difficult times of the pandemic and have been among the first to recover in market value. Leading companies in the industry, such as Apple, Microsoft, Amazon, Facebook, Netflix that have emerged on the market, have known how to exploit IT, to name only the biggest success stories. Startups have also had no problems raising the resources they need, although not all have so far been successful.

In the current context, we must emphasize, once again, the relevance of digitalization, a sine qua non condition for the country to be present in the international market in a competitive way, compatible with its dimension and its industrial park, as we have pointed out in other parts of our text. Less paper, more digital processes!

In all seminars and meetings, I have attended mainly during 2020, I witnessed many debates about the consequences on the world economic picture when Covid-19 is defeated, and vaccines are efficient and equitably distributed.

The common point in these meetings, presented in different countries and by experts from different fields of knowledge, statesmen, economists, etc., is that digitalization has become an inexorable process.

The situation was aggravated after the Ukrainian war, when a complex situation emerged with the United States and Europe supplying war materiel to help the Ukrainians to resist Russian invasion. The Ukrainian reaction was substantial and confounded expectations of a quick resolution to the conflict.

---

11 Available at: https://pt.wikipedia.org/wiki/Francis_Bacon.

Chapter 5

MERCOSUR: THE SOUTHERN COMMON MARKET

Background

Starting in the 1940s, several regional integrationist organizations were created in Latin America. The Economic Commission for Latin America in 1948, the Latin American Free Trade Association in 1960, the Special Commission for Latin American Coordination (Cecla) in 1963, the Institute for the Integration of Latin America (Intal) in 1964, the Caribbean Community (Caricom) in 1973, the Latin American Economic System (Sela) in 1975 and the Latin American Integration Association (Aladi) in 1980.

These and other more recent ones (Unasur, for example) have faced different obstacles, not achieving the results they proposed, for a variety of reasons, among them: international economic crises that had an impact in the region, not to mention our own crises, and periods of economic stagnation that hit us on different occasions. The purposes of these organizations were not always clearly defined. Some have formed large bureaucracies, employing many functionaries, and have distanced themselves from their initial objectives. They also imported different economic policies that were applied by different governments. It is also worth pointing out that in moments of crisis, some organizations, which should suggest or coordinate policies that, as a whole, would help to face and mitigate different crises, have not fulfilled this objective. We have seen each country trying to solve its own problems, without coordinated efforts with its neighbors.

The embryo of Mercosur seems to have been Argentina's initiative to form a "southern bloc" comprising Brazil and the countries of the River Plate Basin. The representatives of these countries met in February 1941, in the Uruguayan border city of Rivera, in order to discuss the creation of a regional customs bloc. In fact, a few months after the historic Rivera meeting, Brazil and Argentina signed a trade treaty in Buenos Aires in which the two countries affirmed their willingness to create a free trade regime that would allow them to achieve a customs union, open to the adhesion of bordering countries.

This initiative did not go forward because of the antagonistic positions of Brazil and Argentina during the Inter-American Consultation Conference in Rio de Janeiro, convened after the Japanese attack on Pearl Harbor. At this conference, the Brazilians adopted a pro-allied position and the Argentines a position of ambiguous neutrality, seen as mostly pro-Axis, which seems to have been the beginning of a decades-long period of mutual hostilities and misunderstandings.

Starting in the early 1950s, some attempts were made to reedit what became known as the "ABC Pact," aiming at a political and economic rapprochement between Brazil, Argentina and Chile.

It was only after the end of the military regimes, which dominated these two countries for many years, that the integration process was intensified. The 1985 Iguaçu Declaration and the 1986 Act of Argentine–Brazilian Integration, both signed by the presidents of Argentina, Raúl Alfonsín, and of Brazil, José Sarney, are milestones in the new relations between Brazil and Argentina. The declaration expressed the firm will to accelerate the bilateral integration process, and the minutes established the Economic Integration and Cooperation Program, of a global, flexible and balanced nature, and provided for preferential treatment vis-à-vis third markets.

The Brazil–Argentina integration process began in 1988 with the signing of the Treaty on Integration, Cooperation, and Development, which aimed to consolidate the bilateral integration process by establishing a common economic space within a maximum period of 10 years. This would be achieved by harmonizing customs, trade, agricultural, industrial, transport and communications policies, and by coordinating the monetary, fiscal and exchange rate policies of the two countries.

It is important to note here the launch in June 1990, by U.S. president George Bush, of the *Initiative for the Americas*, an ambitious proposal for the time, for the long-term creation of a hemispheric free trade zone from Alaska to Tierra del Fuego. North American Free Trade Agreement (NAFTA), created at the end of 1992, seems to have been the first step in this direction.

It was the combination of economic necessity and the political will of Brazil and Argentina that caused the deadlines for the integration process, established by the Treaty of Integration, Cooperation and Development of 1988, to be halved through the signing of the Act of Buenos Aires on 6 July 1990.

Until that date, the integration process of the Southern Cone was developed on a strictly bilateral basis, although Uruguay was invited to and participated in all relevant meetings between the Brazilian and Argentine governments.

It was after the signing of the Act of Buenos Aires that Uruguay entered the new regional compact, soon to be followed by Paraguay.

The signature of the Treaty of Asunción, on 26 March 1991, by the presidents of Argentina, Brazil, Paraguay and Uruguay, established the form of the economic-commercial relations between the four countries, during the transition period 1991/1994, until the full emergence of the Southern Common Market—Mercosur. The Treaty of Asunción entered into force on 29 November of the same year, after being ratified by the legislative powers of every member country.

The agreement reached on the Common External Tariff and other pending issues in the beginning of the second semester of 1994 enabled the presidents of Argentina, Brazil, Paraguay and Uruguay, namely Carlos Menem, Itamar Franco, Juan Carlos Wasmosy and Luis Alberto Lacalle to ratify on 5 August 1994, five hundred years after the signing of the Treaty of Tordesillas, the implementation of Mercosur, starting with a customs union, as of January 1995.

The main objective foreseen by the Asunción Treaty was the enlargement of the national markets of its members, through integration, to accelerate economic development, with social justice. This goal is to be achieved by making more effective use of available resources, preserving the environment, improving physical interconnections, coordinating macroeconomic policies and complementing the different sectors of the economy. The competitive insertion of its four members in the world economy and the scientific and technological development of its members were also considered important.

The constitution of a common market, called the Common Market of the South, according to the Asunción Treaty, implied:

- the free movement of goods, services and productive factors between countries, mainly through the elimination of customs duties and nontariff restrictions and any other measure having equivalent effect;
- the establishment of a common external tariff and the adoption of a common commercial policy with regard to third states or group of states, as well as the coordination of positions in regional and international economic and trade forums;
- the coordination of macroeconomic and sectoral policies among the member states—foreign trade, agricultural, industrial, fiscal, monetary, foreign exchange and capital flows, services, customs, transport and communications and others that may be agreed—in order to ensure adequate conditions of competition between the States Parties; and
- the commitment of the States Parties to harmonize their legislation, in the relevant areas, to achieve the strengthening of the integration process.

The additional protocol to the Treaty of Asunción on the institutional structure of Mercosur was signed in Ouro Preto on 16 December 1994.

Subsequently, the first outlines of a Customs Union were formed, later with the entry into force, on 1 January 1995, of the Common External Tariff (Tarifa Externa Comum).

Therefore, the Ouro Preto Protocol effectively laid the foundations of legal personality, giving it the competencies to negotiate on its own behalf, making agreements with third countries, groups of countries and international organizations.

An important later milestone of Mercosur was the so-called Olivos Protocol, signed in that city, with the aim of solving controversies and minimizing possible differences.

Unlike the European bloc (European Union), the integration of the South American countries has gained strength not because of a war threat, the motivating source of the European blocs, but because of the economic threat. United we would be stronger in the regional associations or trade agreements then envisioned.

Apart from this aspect, I believe that in the case of Brazil and Argentina we also had a strong political component. The rulers involved in the process were sensitive to the political moment that had preceded them, when military groups took power. They thus wanted this alliance to be a protection mechanism against interventionism. They thus sought to strengthen the democratic regimes in their respective countries and protect themselves against authoritarian situations that they had experienced.

It is worth to remember that the idea of a South American Free Trade Area (ALCSA) was a response of the countries in the region to the announcement of the creation of the NAFTA, eventually succeeded by the United States–Mexico–Canada Agreement.

Could the concept that our region should have common policies in different policy areas, and particularly in foreign trade, made perfect sense. In a world that increasingly favors the politics of trading blocs and the coordinated defense of common interests, ALCSA would make sense.

However, ALCSA never came close to fulfilling its objectives and was practically discontinued. If it wasn't moving forward before, post-Covid-19 it appears almost completely stuck in the short and medium terms.

This current vision differs substantially from the one I defended in an article written with Alberto Pfeifer for the book organized by Mário Marconini *A Política Externa Brasileira em Perspectiva: Segurança, Comércio e Relações Bilaterais.*[1]

---

1 Lex/Aduaneiras: 2006.

Entitled "South American Policy," our article is the result of a discussion that allowed us to identify explanatory variables or operational categories for Brazilian action in the region: (1) aspects concerning the state and Brazil's leadership action, (2) Mercosur as central to the advanced exercise of Brazil's South American policy, (3) the regional space of action: the conceptual reference of the Southern frontier vis-à-vis Latin America and (4) the quality of democracy and its effective results for the population and its regional security policy.

The natural Brazilian leadership has sometimes made sense because of our territorial size, as well as the size of our industrial base, our leadership in agriculture and our sophistication in the services area.

I remember well that, although these factors were considered, when it came to the final decision, the issue of sovereignty was the impeding factor when we had to come to a decision. We should not forget that when Brazil was looking for a permanent seat in the United Nations Security Council, Argentines did not support this aspiration.

As mentioned elsewhere in the text, in moments of crisis, we will not unite (as was demonstrated in the pandemic), as well as because of difficulties of a financial nature and of ideological order and long-term interests. Never in the recent past has Latin America been as far apart as it is now!

The Free Trade Zone between Brazil and Argentina, which had been considered at different moments in the political history of these countries, was officially launched in 1986 by Presidents Alfonsín and Sarney, with Uruguay joining in 1989. Paraguay requested to join in 1991. Let's remember that in its origin, the political and strategic component was predominant.

Received with some skepticism by businessmen and politicians in the four countries, Mercosur initially surprised by its commercial dynamism. Helped by Argentina's 1992 convertibility plan, which reactivated the Argentinean economy and acted as a strong inducer of imports, intra-regional trade showed clear signs of growth. Brazilian entrepreneurs have found an Argentinean buyer market, or in different products, we have been identified as a reliable source of supply by our neighbors.

When this initial momentum showed signs of fatigue, it was our turn, in 1994, with the introduction of the Real Plan, to reactivate the trade relationship and also reciprocal investments. Helped by the appreciation of the Real against the dollar, the Argentineans have expanded their sales to our country, accumulating trade surpluses. Between 1990 and 1998, interregional trade within Mercosur increased eightfold, while intraregional trade also expanded, but not at the same rate. Since then, due to successive crises, the trade relationship has deteriorated and, as we have indicated, it has not been possible or feasible to have coordinated policies to address external challenges.

The good commercial results were followed by reciprocal investments that exceeded US$ 8 billion until the critical phase in 2001.

This initial success is perhaps one of the reasons for the later difficulties. What was missing was the continuity of an agenda that, besides implementing measures agreed upon in treaties or multilateral meetings, would also lay a more solid foundation to consolidate the initial successful effort. For example, macroeconomic convergence, an important condition for this consolidation, remained at the level of good intentions.

In the absence of economic growth, external crises aggravated the internal picture. Disputes between countries have become an increasingly important item on diplomats' agendas. It was not rare that the highest levels, especially in Brazil and Argentina, had to intervene to calm tempers, seeking palliative solutions to prevent further deterioration. The crises in Asian countries in the 1980s have contaminated the so-called emerging countries, especially in Latin America. Brazil was hit with a substantial loss of foreign exchange reserves, a reflection of the climate of distrust regarding the sustainability of our economic policy.

Unable to perform a competitive devaluation, the Argentineans, particularly in the sectors most affected by Brazilian exports, began to pressure their government to take protectionist measures, intensifying the dispute between the two countries. Unilateral protectionist measures were implemented that made trade relations more difficult. In a way, this scenario repeated itself in 2019, when at its end, and after the inauguration of Alberto Fernandez, the Argentine congress approved a set of protectionist measures, seeking to solve the severe currency crisis, soaring inflation, unemployment and lack of growth.

As always, the sectors that felt aggrieved, or at a competitive disadvantage, publicly expressed their discontent. Past benefits and achievements are forgotten, as are strategic advantages regarding the future.

With the foreign exchange crisis and the policy put in place to solve it, the bilateral relationship deteriorated even further. From these difficult months, I highlight the greater sensitivity of the private sector and the demonstration of Brazilian solidarity with the Argentineans.

What has become transparent in different crises is that the perceptions of Mercosur's importance can be rather different. The Argentine perception is that the Brazilian market is what counts primarily. The position of Uruguay and Paraguay is similar, given the dependence of their economies on Brazil. We Brazilians have a more strategic vision because we understand that, in a globalized world economy, where economic blocks are dominant forces, we are stronger as Mercosur, which has been valued externally. In any case, the

Argentine market has always been of great relevance for the Brazilian industrial sector, and prominently our largest market in Latin America.

This is why we must undertake, private sector and government alike, a great effort to consolidate and relaunch Mercosur.

The manifestations of different Brazilian authorities are positive, in the sense that Mercosur must continue to be a priority in Brazilian foreign policy. A growing number of politicians and businessmen converged in this direction. The crisis in Argentina, and to a lesser extent in Brazil, should bring us closer. Ideologies aside, geography makes an association between Argentina and Brazil fundamental. We must analyze this moment and take a step forward. Argentina and Brazil are indelibly associated. It is not an option, but rather a necessity for harmonious coexistence.

The Latin American Business Council—CEAL, created in 1990, presented the governments of Mercosur member countries and their neighbors with a series of documents in 2004 containing proposals for action aimed at strengthening the regional bloc. Several of these suggestions were accepted and implemented, showing the consistency between Ceal's strategic thinking and the attitudes of national governments.

In the case of Mercosur, several commitments have been maintained, despite the difficult situations faced at various times by its members. At the political level, members remain committed to the democratic rule of law and to the bloc's internal cohesion, aimed at joint negotiations with third parties and expansion to South American neighbors. At the institutional level, by a growing, gradual and controlled process of delegation of functional attributions to appropriate people and spheres. In the infrastructure aspect, adding efforts directed to the rationalization of logistics, energy supply and the creation of a communications network. On the economic level, through the search for macroeconomic harmonization and coordination, and by seeking to strengthen the common external tariff.

Mercosur must not be seen only as a governmental creation of the late 1980s, nor as an exclusively state-led project. Mercosur's regional integration must be seen as an ever wider initiative of the citizens of member countries.

I advocate that there should be no discontinuity, but rather the deepening of the customs union and eventual discussion, aiming at the constitution of the Common Market; the improvement of joint negotiation procedures with third parties; the resumption of the Reciprocal Credit Agreement; the legal, fiscal and financial facilitation of productive integration development; the harmonization of agricultural and livestock health surveillance; greater macroeconomic approximation; the increase of energy and physical integration; the implementation of common sustainable development policies.

It is essential to learn from experience. The reduction in growth has revealed the asymmetry of Mercosur's evolution: initially a lot of commerce, some investment, not enough institutions. Regional integration is a process of institution building, not of institutes, and it must have the full political support of the respective societies. For example, one does not want a Mercosur tribunal, but an effective mechanism for the settlement of trade disputes.

The agenda of the third stage, that of the Common Market, must be considered in light of the political–economic framework of the main countries of the agreement. It should:

- Increase social participation;
- Consolidate democratic principles and the rule of law;
- Seek rational and sustained exploitation of natural resources;
- Facilitate mutual support and solidarity in the face of adverse economic impacts;
- Operationalize the bloc's unique interface with other countries, regions and international organizations;
- Make clear the political commitment to the deepening and expansion of the bloc, with a single currency, the free flow of products and production factors, and joint external integration;
- Strengthen the project's institutionality and supranationality, giving Mercosur its own identity and a greater range of action.

Let's register some initiatives, or even emphasize/consolidate policies that should be implemented:

Strategically:
1. Continue to insist on convergence of foreign policies, acting jointly, when possible, in international political negotiations of the member countries, and avoiding unilateral practices as much as possible;
2. Promote measures that lead to the growth of Bolivia and Chile's political and economic participation in Mercosur;
3. With the countries of the Andean Community, the ultimate goal should be to form a politically and physically integrated free trade zone between the countries of South America, the original idea of ALCSA;
4. Seek the adoption of common negotiating strategies and tactics involving all South American countries, especially vis-à-vis the Pacific Alliance;
5. Define and implement common Mercosur strategies for political and economic action to increase cooperation and trade with Central American, Caribbean, Asian and African countries.

Institutionally:

1. In the commercial plan, the adoption of the "Mercosur" brand, next to the mark of the country where the good was finished, for all products involving production steps covering at least two countries in the region;
2. Incorporate clear provisions tending to enhance the international personality earned by Mercosur as a political and economic partner of groups of countries that form it;
3. That the governments take a pragmatic and realistic look at the issue of Mercosur's institutionalization, in order to clearly signal, at the institutional level and in Mercosur's internal and external dialogue, a commitment to the consolidation of the bloc and to its consistent and coordinated participation in the negotiating forums to which it belongs;
4. In terms of infrastructure, accelerate physical and energy integration, with the participation of international organizations and foreign companies (joint projects);
5. At the academic level, to encourage Brazilian universities to have active cooperation projects with South American universities and bilateral language communication;
6. Seek to integrate information technology (IT) and AI projects between specialized agencies and research institutes in the region;
7. At the social level, implement intergovernmental projects that enable effective intra-bloc cooperation, aimed at reducing asymmetries between the parties and social inequality, through, for example, the extension of Brazilian vaccination programs, and programs to stimulate early childhood education in Paraguay and Bolivia;

Economically:

1. Enable the effective implementation and use of dispute settlement mechanisms in Mercosur, either through the use of an Arbitration Court, or by encouraging the private settlement of disputes;
2. Establish intergovernmental zoo- and phytosanitary control and inspection mechanisms, responsible for rule making and dispute settlement, including associate members;
3. Facilitate business at the intra-regional level, especially by reducing bureaucratic procedures for trade in goods. Encourage corporate *joint ventures* to mitigate perverse competitive effects between different producers of the same articles or goods;
4. Use mechanisms to finance production that facilitate intra- and extra-Mercosur trade;
5. Guarantee BNDES's support to Brazilian companies that are willing to operate in Mercosur countries and in Latin America in general.

In 2003, under the inspiration of President Fernando Henrique Cardoso, at the XX Meeting of the Common Market Council held in Buenos Aires, and with the approval of all partners, a group with a diverse composition was suggested and approved, including businessmen, academics and members of their respective governments, to undertake a critical analysis of Mercosur and to make a forward-looking reflection on its functioning. Twenty-eight personalities were invited to prepare a text with their points of view on Mercosur's situation and its future.

The results of this meeting were recorded in a book in 2003, with 496 pages, with the contributions received and the conclusions reached by those who were able to participate in the conclusive meeting held in Rio de Janeiro.

The date chosen was also symbolic, because on 30 November 1985, as mentioned earlier, Presidents Alfonsín and Sarney held the first meeting between the two countries for the founding of Mercosur.

Obviously, summarizing almost 500 pages is not an easy exercise, but I believe that they complement and bring into focus the most relevant themes for all those who want to dive into the main challenges of Mercosur and, therefore, I believe that the goals of the book were met.

1. Consolidation of the Customs Union—most of the authors consider the effort to preserve and consolidate it a priority, because it represents a diplomatic attitude that strengthens Mercosur externally and a fundamental instrument for the continuation of the integration project;
2. Improving Mercosur's institutional structure—with some of the participants suggesting the creation of a body that would adopt the European Union model;
3. To promote the strengthening of the legal security of the approved norms, some authors suggest legal or constitutional reforms to seek to overcome the legal-institutional and regional problems of law;
4. In the social area, they agree on the need to foster greater cooperation in the implementation of projects to combat unemployment and poverty, within a context that goes beyond the economic-commercial dimension of Mercosur;
5. Coordination of macroeconomic policies imposed by the international framework, even acknowledging the great complexity, and the requirement that gradualist policies must be adopted;
6. Financing joint projects, with funds made available for these projects and, if possible, credit lines in favor of smaller members. Infrastructure projects are also recommended as a way to reduce transportation costs and increase competitiveness vis-à-vis third markets;

7. External relationship—the relationship between the integration process and the major economic-trade negotiations must have Mercosur's active participation, even considering the difficulties of negotiating as a bloc in the face of the complexity of the external situation;

8. The Covid-19 pandemic changed many of the considerations recorded in the book. The first signs at the end of April and the beginning of May were no more favorable, as the consequences of the new coronavirus affected the different Mercosur countries differently. As a member of the Argentine group commented, when Brazil has a flu, its neighbors get pneumonia. In any case, a possible cooperation between the countries is extremely dependent on the posture of the presidents of Brazil and Argentina, who have to leave ideologies aside and seek common ground for the benefit of their countries.

The default on foreign debt starting in 2019 has aggravated the case of Argentina, which has defaulted for the ninth time. The negotiations with the creditors resulted in an agreement.

Given the Covid-19 pandemic scenario, on 4 May 2020[2] Argentina's president announced that he will no longer participate in new international agreements, with the exception of the two most important agreements under discussion with the European Union and the European Free Trade Association.[3]

Argentina's decision to abandon the Mercosur negotiations should not affect the automotive agreement with Argentina,[4] renegotiated in September 2019. In any case, there was no unanimity among diplomats about whether Argentina's decision will actually be a facilitator in the Common External Tariff discussions, which only time will tell.

In an interview with *Valor* newspaper, published on 12 February 2020, EU ambassador in Brasília Ignacio Ibañez indicated that the trade agreement is on "stand by," waiting for concrete actions from the Brazilian government to combat deforestation and fires, as well as proactive measures in sustainability policies. He acknowledges that there have been notable changes in the executive's behavior, but deforestation has reached the highest level since 2008. In any case, his message was positive, even understanding the challenges within the European community itself—a certain division among its members.

---

2 Available at: http://glo.bo/3k4o43q.
3 Switzerland, Norway, Iceland and Liechtenstein.
4 Available at: http://glo.bo/2Nl2LyF.

Another positive sign was the visit to Brazil of Xiana Méndez, Spanish economist, who is the main advisor of socialist Pedro Sánchez for commercial matters. She was incisive in her assessment that, for the Spanish, there is no chance of opening the negotiations, using the issue of deforestation as a pretext, despite the reticence that appears either from governments or, sometimes, from Parliament, which are reflections of public opinion but also mask protectionist interests. In November he proposed in a letter his position in favor of the agreement to be sanctioned. These are positive signs that encourage us.

Uruguay's position is to increasingly defend a position of autonomy to conclude trade agreements independent of Mercosur.

Another issue is the Common External Tariff, always very controversial.

The election of Lula, on 30 October 2022, and his long-standing relationship with Argentina, and with President Alberto Fernandez, creates the expectation that the two countries will pursue common objectives that are essential for their future and also the future of Mercosur. For that, the Mercosur–EU Trade Agreement is of upmost importance. We must overcome our differences with our neighbors, and Brazil has to establish a policy in the Amazon that serves our interests as well as those of the rest of the world.

Historically, Lula's relations with all Latin American countries have always been positive and constructive.

In his initial declarations, Lula made it very clear that among his priorities will be the return to our past "status" with our neighbors.

Chapter 6

BRAZIL–U.S. RELATIONS:
A LONG-TERM PARTNERSHIP

Brazil–U.S. Relations in the Latin America Context

Before a discussion about the central theme of this chapter, which will address the changes in the international scene with the inauguration of Joseph Biden, a historical overview of the relationship between the United States and Latin America seemed opportune, particularly as far as Brazil is concerned.

The selected documents and facts are as follows:

- Monroe Doctrine—1823–1920;
- Roosevelt Corollary—1904;
- Brazil–U.S. Joint Commission—1950;
- Alliance for Progress—1961;
- Rockefeller Report of the Americas—Document published by the *New York Times* reporting on the official mission of the President of the Republic to the Western Hemisphere—by Nelson Rockefeller—1965—It deals with the full text of the controversial and somewhat surprising Rockefeller Mission that visited to 20 nations in America;
- Brazil Task Force—United States—elaborated by an independent task force sponsored by CEBRI—Brazilian Center for International Relations—August 2002.

Monroe Doctrine

The so-called Monroe Doctrine was announced by U.S. president James Monroe (president from 1817 to 1825) in his message to Congress on 2 December 1823.

> We take this opportunity to state, as a principle affecting the rights and interests of the United States, that the American continents, by virtue of the free and independent condition they have acquired and retain, can

no longer be considered, in the future, as susceptible to colonization by any European power.

(Message from President James Monroe to the U.S. Congress, 1823)

The phrase that sums up the doctrine is, "America for Americans."
His policies consisted of three points:

- the non-creation of new colonies in the Americas;
- nonintervention in the internal affairs of American countries;
- the nonintervention of the United States in conflicts related to European countries such as wars between these countries and their colonies.

At the time, the Monroe Doctrine represented a serious warning not only to the Holy Alliance, but also to Great Britain itself[1] (with whom the Americans had recently fought the War of 1812), although its immediate effect, as to the defense of the new American states, was purely moral, given that the United States' economic interests and political and military capabilities at the time did not extend beyond the Caribbean region. It is very important to note that the United States at that time was still far from being considered even a regional power. Anyway, the formulation of the doctrine helped Britain thwart European plans to recolonize America and allowed the United States to continue to expand its borders westward, the doctrine became an important reference when discussing the North American relationship with the countries of our region.

Expansionist Policy

From the end of the nineteenth century, the United States gave an imperialistic character to the Monroe Doctrine and began to strengthen their military, economic and political influence in the Caribbean region, including through military interventions. The goal was to turn this Caribbean Sea into a mare nostrum because of its strategic importance.

Between 1891 and 1912, the United States carried out a series of military interventions: 1891, Haiti; 1895, Nicaragua; 1898, Puerto Rico and Cuba; 1899, Nicaragua; 1902, Venezuela; 1903, Dominican Republic and Colombia; 1904, Dominican Republic and Guatemala; 1906, Cuba; 1907, Dominican

---

1 The Holy Alliance was a coalition uniting the great monarchist powers of Austria, Prussia and Russia.

Republic; 1910, Nicaragua; 1910–1911, Honduras; 1912, Cuba, Nicaragua and the Dominican Republic (outside the Caribbean, military action is taken against Chile in 1891).

Roosevelt Corollary

The Roosevelt Corollary was a foreign policy postulate, in addition to the Monroe Doctrine, authored by the president of the United States Theodore Roosevelt. Combined with the "Big Stick" Policy, the corollary was the hallmark of a period of increased U.S. control over Latin American countries.

The Roosevelt Corollary was expressed in the President's 1904 Annual Message to the U.S. Congress. The United States declared itself willing to militarily occupy countries that were experiencing a crisis due to their foreign debt. In the message, Roosevelt expressed his conviction that a nation that can maintain order and fulfill its obligations need not fear interference from the United States. However, a "civilized nation" like the United States would have to assume the role of "world policeman" and be forced to intervene in case the bonds of civilized society in other countries weaken.

Franklin Roosevelt's "Good Neighbor" policy[2] was formulated in a completely different context than before, forcing the United States to change policy. The great crisis of 1929 forced Americans to seek new markets where they could export industrial products, thus opening markets to help the U.S. economy, badly shaken by the depression of the 1930s.

In 1943, President Roosevelt met with President Getúlio Vargas in Natal (RN) to discuss Brazil's participation in World War II. At that time our president negotiated loans in order to modernize the Brazilian industrial park. At first, Brazil declared itself neutral in the conflict and later joined the Allies when several Brazilians ships were sunk off our coast. Brazil sent a small expeditionary force that played an important role in Italy, particularly in the Battle of Monte Castello.

Brazil–U.S. Joint Commission

Formed within the Ministry of Finance, and integrated by Brazilian and North American technicians, the Brazil–U.S. Joint Commission on Economic Development was the result of negotiations between Brazil and the United States that began in 1950, during the Dutra government, aimed

---

2 The Good Neighbor policy was launched by President Roosevelt during the Pan-American Conference in Montevideo in December 1933.

at financing a program to reequip the infrastructure sectors of the Brazilian economy. The commission was officially established on 19 July 1951 and closed on 31 July 1953. It was part of the North American technical assistance plan for Latin America known as Point IV, made public in 1949, when a commission composed of Eugênio Gudin, Otávio Gouveia de Bulhões and Valder Lima Sarmanho was formed in Brazil to study the priorities for a development program for the country. This commission ended up prioritizing the agriculture, energy and transport sectors, without, however, formulating a specific financing project.

In April 1950 the idea arose to create the Joint Commission, and in the middle of the negotiations, in the month of October, Getúlio Vargas was elected president. In December, his future minister of Foreign Affairs, João Neves da Fontoura, was appointed to negotiate in the United States the outstanding points for the implementation of the commission. That same month the agreement to form the commission was sealed. Based on previous understandings, Brazil was willing to continue exporting some strategic minerals to the United States, in particular manganese and monazite sands. In his work, the Joint Commission made use of studies on the Brazilian economy previously prepared by the American missions Cooke and Abbink, sent to Brazil in 1942 and 1948, respectively.

As a result of the work of the Joint Commission it was established that the National Bank for Economic Development (BNDE) would be created, the institution in charge of financing and managing the resources for these projects raised in Brazil or with the American EXIM Bank and the World Bank, responsible for foreign currency financing. BNDE was created on 20 June 1952, by Law No. 1628.[3]

During the Vargas government, only US$181 million was granted by foreign banks and not all projects received financing. In any case, the Joint Commission and the BNDE helped introduce more rational management practices and application of public resources in economic investments in Brazil and contributed to form a team of Brazilian technicians capable of elaborating development projects.

The Joint Commission presented its final report to the minister of finance, Eugênio Gudin, already in the Café Filho government, in November 1954.

---

3   Later, during the Figueiredo administration, its name was changed to Banco Nacional de Desenvolvimento Econômico e Social (BNDES), to include social policies among its objectives.

Alliance for Progress

Its origin dates back to an official proposal by President John F. Kennedy, in his speech on 13 March 1961 during a reception at the White House to Latin American ambassadors.

The Alliance would last 10 years, projecting an investment of US$ 20 billion, mainly the responsibility of the United States, but also from various international organizations, European countries and private companies.

The proposal was then detailed at the meeting held in Punta del Este, Uruguay, 5–27 August, at the OAS Inter-American Economic and Social Council. The Declaration and Charter of Punta del Este were both approved by all countries present.

The Alliance for Progress includes among its objectives to end illiteracy by 1970, make land reform, distribute income, avoid inflation and promote industrialization. Leonel Brizola, then a congressman, demonized the Alliance for Progress and saw it as a battering ram for American interventionist interests.

Initially, the Alliance was enthusiastically received, called the Marshall Plan for Latin America. However, the optimistic mood shown in early 1961 by South American authorities turned into skepticism or total disbelief by mid-1962. South American authorities wanted to receive resources to finance infrastructure and were irritated by American demands that the region make fiscal efforts to keep budgets balanced.

Roberto Campos, former Brazilian minister of planning and also Brazilian ambassador in Washington during João Goulart's term in office, described the local feeling in a letter to a high-ranking U.S. government official dated September 1962, complaining that the United States would only be concerned with the "primacy of stabilization" and not with economic and social development.

Rockefeller Mission

The mission headed by Nelson Aldrich Rockefeller was an initiative of then president Richard Nixon.

Before we go properly into the ambitious goals of the mission, it would be interesting to describe who Nelson Rockefeller was.

As stated on the back cover of the book *The American friend—Nelson Rockefeller and Brazil*, Antônio Tota describes him:

Heir to one of the world's largest fortunes, member of the "liberal" wing of the Republican Party, Nelson Aldrich Rockefeller was governor of

New York State for four terms, vice president of the United States, and eternal aspirant to the first post of the Yankee Republic. But what is revealed in this tasty profile is a lesser known side of his biography: Rockefeller became close to [Brazil] when he became head of the U.S. Office of Inter-American Affairs (which brought Orson Welles and Walt Disney to Brazil, and sent Carmen Miranda the other way), an organization whose mission was to distance the Vargas government from Nazi-fascism and, once World War II was won, to ensure that Brazil would remain in the North American bloc of influence. With hard work, "good intentions" and strongly imbued with the ideology of his country and his class, the politician manifested genuine interest in Brazil, and became involved here, including as a direct investor, patron and entrepreneur, in the most diverse activities, from rubber cultivation to urban planning in São Paulo, from encouraging the arts to setting up investment funds that modernized the local capital market, always in an attempt to import efficiency and the American way of life as antidotes to the expansion of communism.

As for the mission, I have separated some relevant points.

The *New York Times*, prestigious organ of the American press, edited a 144-page pocket booklet that recounts all the details of the mission, from the signing of the letter by the then president, divided into five chapters with the information and data collected during the trip.

Interestingly, before we go into the report's conclusions, I thought it appropriate to comment on the introductory letter by Tad Szulc, Latin America correspondent for that newspaper.

Latin America developed a synthesis—*love/hate* with USA. The Rockefeller report offered specific recommendations on how the United States could in the best way, to assist Latin America to overcome a legacy of many decades of economic and social imbalance.

Going properly into what I consider the conclusion of that mission to Brazil that he headed in the Nixon administration, it is worth mentioning:

In a prefatory letter to President Nixon, Governor Rockefeller does not skirt the issue of demonstrations and violence directed against the America Mission during its visits to several countries. They were, he notes, a manifestation of deep causes, which the United States must work to correct:

1. a general frustration, exacerbated by subversive forces, over the failure to achieve a more rapid improvement in the standard of living
2. blame for the United States because of its identification with the failure of the Alliance for Progress to live up to expectations
3. discontent with the failure of the people's own governments to meet their needs.

I draw attention to "a general frustration exacerbated by strong opposition forces regarding the failure of countries in the region to achieve a faster standard of living."

In the conclusion, the recommendations that I believe with time have not lost their timeliness:

ACTION COURSE

It was in that spirit that this report recommended the reorganization of the United States government's foreign policy structure, fundamental changes in U.S. trade and loan policies, renegotiation of foreign debts and a more realistic division of labor in the hemisphere.

The ability of sovereign nations and free peoples to work together in mutual growth is crucial to survival—and crucial to the quality of life of those who survive.

Achieving such cooperation among the peoples of this hemisphere is the central objective of this report and all of its specific recommendations.

I believe that if he was still alive, Rockefeller would be disappointed with the results achieved so far.

Brazil–U.S. Task Force

In 2002, the Brazilian Center for International Relations (Cebri) sponsored an Independent Task Force to analyze Brazil–U.S. relations, which I coordinated.

The 26-page document, released in August 2002, had an executive summary from which some items are transcribed:

Importance of the United States

The indisputable importance of the United States for Brazil's international relations, amplified from that country's status as the only superpower in the last thirteen years and the imminence of new trade agreements decisive for the future of the national economy, requires a reexamination of bilateral relations and imposes a series of actions aimed at improving their quality in the immediate future. Therefore, to this end, CEBRI has constituted a task force, formed by entrepreneurs, intellectuals, diplomats, politicians, and trade unionists, which presents the following suggestions to Brazilian society and government:

Images and Mutual Perceptions

- Develop strategies to promote Brazil in the press, universities, NGOs, and other North American public and private entities. These strategies should include, in particular, foundations or other public or private institutions dedicated to Latin American and/or Brazilian studies; stimulate contacts with North American people or institutions that are present in Brazil.
- To encourage the teaching and dissemination of information concerning the United States, in order to achieve a better knowledge of that country by Brazil and Brazilians; in particular, the creation of centers specialized in U.S. affairs is recommended.
- Stimulate discussion about the bilateral relationship, in its various aspects, in existing non-governmental organizations.

Multilateralism, Regionalism, Unilateralism

- Seek the support of the United States for multilateralism in all relevant spheres of international relations: terrorism, agricultural liberalization, protectionism, education and technological capacity building, security, and intelligence.
- Make efforts to prevent regionalism from replacing multilateralism as the central priority of U.S. foreign policy. There is no evidence that hemispheric regionalism would result in trade concessions in the areas that are of most interest to Brazil, nor that it would result in better relations in political areas.

Democracy and Reform in the Americas

- Focus the bilateral dialogue on how to make Brazil's internal democratic agenda compatible, which will increasingly turn to social problems, with the post-9/11 U.S. foreign agenda increasingly distancing itself from global social issues.

Defense and Security: A Dialogue

- Propose a dialogue with the United States that includes defense and security issues and others of bilateral interest, thus contributing to adequately dimension the importance of this issue in the relationship between the two countries.

Free Trade: Rhetoric or Commitment

- Deepen criticism of U.S. trade policy, both in terms of protectionism and the lack of commitment by the United States to the multilateral system.
- Prioritize a "proactive" position with Washington, demonstrating its commitment to free but fair and balanced trade. It is necessary to enlighten public opinion in the United States in this regard, possibly by allying with the free-trade and pro-consumer forces in that country.
- Maintain coherence in its claims before the United States, particularly with respect to the importance of Mercosur for its international insertion and the need to avoid its disintegration.

Environment: Beyond the Amazon

- Articulate and act positively in multilateral forums. A defensive policy, such as the one practiced in some of the environmental negotiations, does not reflect the real importance of the country.
- Work more directly with North American civil society organizations involved in protecting and defending the environment, in order to clarify the positions of society and the Brazilian government with respect to environmental issues.

Brazil's Importance to the United States

There is full awareness that the United States is much more important to Brazil than Brazil is to the United States. However, there is also awareness of the international stature that Brazil has acquired in recent years and in particular of the renewed value that influential sectors of public opinion and American society have come to confer on Brazil (as the Council on Foreign Relations' own report on Brazil shows). It would not be an exaggeration to say that Brazil and the Brazilian elite are watching for any signs of recognition from other countries, and particularly on the part of the United States, of the progress the country has made in the recent past. Besides this, one of the greatest Brazilian frustrations continues to be a certain North American apathy about Brazil's "historical" value to the United States (for example, our participation in World War II and the Brazilian initiative in the hemispheric context to legitimize the US campaign in Afghanistan following the 11 September terrorist attacks):

It is indisputable that the Brazilian influence over the USA is many times less than the American influence in Brazil. Even in comparison to the importance that other national cultures have for the USA, it is undeniable that it is much lower than in Western European countries (such as Italy, Ireland, Germany) or even the Americas (such as Mexico). But it is also necessary to recognize that it is not negligible, it has been increasing and tends to grow even more.

The number of Brazilians who live and work—in conditions of immigration regularity or not—has experienced continuous growth since the mid-1980s, when economic and political crises made Brazil, for the first time in its history, a nation with a significant number of emigrants. In some regions of the U.S., such as the Miami neighborhoods, areas of New Jersey close to New York, Boston (where they add to the traditional local Portuguese community), San Francisco and Greater Washington, Brazilians are already an important group of workers and entrepreneurs. In some of these places, Portuguese is already taught as an elective subject in public schools.

The long-standing presence of Brazilian popular music—especially bossa nova, which influenced many American artists over four decades—in the American cultural scene is also on the rise: more and more Brazilian musicians are performing in concert halls in the USA, dozens there have taken root and are successful in influential circles and receive awards of recognized merit, radio and cable TV programs are dedicated to MPB. The situation is similar when it comes to cinema, with the better distribution of Brazilian films in specialized circuits and the appearance of filmmakers and actors from the country in the lists of finalists for expressive awards. The popularization of soccer in American society, especially among children and adolescents, has also made Brazil better known and admired among ordinary citizens in the USA, given the country's unquestionable leadership in this sport. The efforts of some Brazilian cultural animators have also made Brazil appear as never before in the US fine arts market, including mega exhibitions in top museums, such as the Guggenheim in New York in 2001.

Between 1996 and 2001, several new centers for Brazilian studies were inaugurated in prestigious academic institutions in the USA (Stanford University, Georgetown University, Pittsburgh University, Columbia University and Woodrow Wilson International Center for Scholars), which is likely to help improve the understanding of Brazil's importance among opinion makers in the USA.

- There is consensus on the need to know what we want and to demand from the United States what we want. Our relations with the United States are presumably very good; however, we have yet to define what these good relations consist of, what its strengths are and where there are weaknesses that can be transformed to better serve the national interest.
- The lack of attention to Brazil that is perceived in American foreign policy is partly due to mistaken images and perceptions about that country; is also due, however, to the place Brazil occupies in the United States' list of strategic priorities—always very much centered on defense and national security issues and, only in a second moment, focused on commercial or economic issues. Brazil does not represent any threat to the national or regional security of the United States and therefore remains marginal from the point of view of U.S. priority interests—unlike countries such as Cuba, Colombia, Panama, Venezuela, Nicaragua or El Salvador (although in different historical contexts).
- Traditionally, Brazil could be portrayed as a latecomer in the process of international insertion. Perhaps for the first time Brazil now has the opportunity to catch up and participate fully in the process of global integration, inserting itself in a way that reflects its real interests, its real stature, and its real potential. Brazil is present and active in a number of global issues, choosing to act as a bloc in an environment of increasing influence of global governance values, despite economic and political difficulties of all kinds.
- The coincidence of common visions and characteristics of Brazil and the United States as democracies that promote economic growth, economic integration, and peaceful relations is recognized by authorities in both countries. Brazil has every interest in forging a strong alliance with the United States in order to support democratic leaders and resist the authoritarian temptations that threaten to resurface on the South American continent. The role of Brazil, Mercosur, and Brazil in Mercosur,

especially when we remember that it was Brazil that suggested
and promoted the adoption of the "Democratic Clause" in the
ambit of the bloc, should be taken into consideration as a central
strategic element in this alliance.

- Portuguese is establishing itself as a widespread language on the
East Coast of the United States, where about 0.7 million Brazilians
live, concentrated in states such as Florida, New York, New
Jersey, Connecticut, and Massachusetts, the largest contingent of
Brazilians in a region outside of Brazil.

- Brazilian arts, especially music, are among the foreign
cultural manifestations most welcomed in the North American
environment; it is also worth mentioning a greater presence of
Brazilian cinema in the North American audiovisual market in
the recent past.

In this historical appreciation of the relationship between the United States
and Latin America, I did not refer to the more recent past.

However, what has become evident in the last decades were periods of
alternation in which our government was close to Washington at times and
distant and even unfriendly in others.

Interestingly, the personal relationship between President Bolsonaro and
Donald Trump played an important role when it came to personal empathy,
but with no political results.

In the past, the military governments had a good relationship with the
United States. A comment, never denied, by Juracy Magalhães, minister
of foreign affairs in the Castelo Branco government: "What is good for the
United States is good for Brazil."

But Juscelino Kubitschek had problems with the International Monetary
Fund (IMF) regarding the condition of his monetary policy. Jânio Quadros
spent a short time in power (decorating Che Guevara), and João Goulart was
not hostile to the Americans, although his government, committed in the
view of many political groups to greater state intervention in the economy,
did not have Uncle Sam's blessing.

After redemocratization we had some ups and downs.

José Sarney was not an internationalist and had little rapprochement with
the United States.

Fernando Collor de Mello was his successor, but during his time in power,
until his impeachment, he had a pro-American attitude, and his ministers
were all well connected with the United States.

Itamar Franco was present at the meeting to launch the Free Trade Area
of the Americas—FTAA (that didn't work out), accompanied by Fernando

States. The defined team was very well received, with people experienced in public management, such as Janet Yellen as the treasury secretary, who met with full approval (she was on the Federal Reserve Board).

For Biden, the election of Democrats in two Senate seats by the State of Georgia is crucial to the functioning of his government, giving him the majority in two Houses.

Anyway, the feeling is that the policies that will be adopted will not be hostile to Brazil, even though our president has declared himself an admirer of Trump, and even delayed the recognition of his victory at the polls. The historical relationship between the two countries is far above institutional and personal interests.

The repercussions on the Brazilian economy, especially on our foreign policy, during the Bolsonaro administration were not well received at the beginning of his term, but it has changed afterward. Certainly, the war in Ukraine will continue to be a sticking point in our relations. Also, it will be of great importance who will be indicated by Lula as our chancellor. During his two mandates, Lula had a good and fair relationship with Washington and is expected to continue to do so in his third term.

In the United States what we saw was Trump throwing accusations without any proof of fraud in the electoral process, unprecedented in American politics, thus setting a bad example for the rest of the world. One of the characteristics of a populist leader like Trump is to have the gift of leading voters to ignore facts and not support measures that are not in line with his political goals.

Political analyst Francis Fukuyama, highly respected in the United States and the democratic world, in an interview with the *Globo*, 3 November 2020, commented that "Trump has challenged the rule of law like no other, posing challenge to the institutions."

Thus, observers of world politics have reflected that regardless of which president is chosen, the United States will continue to have great weight in world economics and politics.

The national and international press, even before Biden's election result, made it clear that Brazil seems not to be the pariah that our chancellor would like, according to his statement in October, during the training of new diplomats. He will have to make clear his commitments to the preservation of the Amazon forest. In fact, in recent months, we have already observed a change in the country's posture in this regard.

Another point that will be on Biden's agenda, and which has always been present in Democratic Party governments, is the question of human rights (I remember the differences between Jimmy Carter and the Geisel government) as well as the ever-sensitive issue of labor law and, of course, corruption. It is worth remembering that in the trade agreements made by the United States with countries in the region, as in the case of NAFTA, Chile and Central American countries, these have always been relevant points. Many analysts understood that it would be one of the fundamental obstacles for the viability of the FTAA. The countries of the region would reject these American demands.

When Dilma Rousseff was impeached in September 2016, the person who spoke out on behalf of the United States was then vice president Biden, recognizing that the process had taken place in accordance with the Brazilian Constitution and the assumption of power by Vice President Michel Temer, who at his inauguration declared: "Brazil will continue to be one of the closest U.S. partners in the region, because in democracies partnerships are not based on the relationship between 2 leaders, but on the long lasting relationship between the two countries."

Conclusion

Before I get properly into the final comments, it would be interesting to disclose my personal perspective in relation to the United States. My generation was strongly influenced by its values, culture and open democracy, which have been a source of inspiration for many countries in the region and adopted by the vast majority.

In my specific case, I would add that my father, a civil engineer, graduated from the University of Michigan in 1924, and my mother, fluent in English, worked at the Rockefeller Foundation's office in Rio. Therefore, I had at home a background that was influenced by American culture and customs. I loved American music, as did many of my generation, admirers of Frank Sinatra, Ella Fitzgerald, Sarah Vaughan, Nat King Cole, Count Basie (who I saw play in NY), Chet Baker, Billy Eckstine, Billie Holiday, and many others. In the cinema I was an unconditional fan of Doris Day, Katharine Hepburn, Lauren Bacall, Marilyn Monroe, not to extend myself too much further.

Professionally, after graduating, I worked for two years at Citibank (then First National City Bank), one of the few accredited and operating in Rio. From there I left in 1958 to work at Deltec, founded by North American professionals (Dauphinot, Archer and David Beaty III) who sought to implement capital market techniques in Brazil. They were pioneers in the work of encouraging companies to go public, forming a base of Brazilian shareholders to consolidate democratic capitalism in the country. The assumption was that popular capitalism and appropriate governance between the controlling and minority shareholders would strengthen the democratic regime. This concept, from the beginning, attracted me, because this formulation of a basis of democratization of capital would strengthen the market economy and keep us away from the "siren song," of those who preached a predominant regime with the presence of the state, not to mention those who were very much in favor of a socialist regime. Deltec, discreet but effective, has always supported all manifestations in favor of the market economy, and this was the institution to which I was professionally linked for many years before accepting the invitation to structure the Brazilian Securities Commission— CVM in 1977. Having graduated from the National Faculty of Economic Sciences (University of Brazil), my higher education was strongly influenced by my then professors: Roberto Campos, Octavio Bulhões, Antônio Dias Leite, Paulo Lyra and Casimiro Ribeiro, among others, liberal training that created the foundations of open democratic regimes and market economy.

Subsequently, as president of the Latin American Business Council— CEAL, and with frequent visits and meetings with businesspeople in our region, I could see that, despite all the possible blemishes, the democratic regime associated to an open economy completely surpassed the possible alternatives on our continent.

This long preamble was to make it clear that there was, by training or conviction, no anti-American bias, but quite the opposite: a deep respect and admiration for what the American people have achieved.

In recent years my admiration for our northern neighbors was affected, under Donald Trump's administration, especially when it comes to social issues. Income inequality in the country is one of the main issues; the treatment of Latino immigrants and the way their children were treated; the racial issue that was largely evidenced in different police episodes, as well as the lack of opportunities for its citizens to ascend the social ladder, not to mention the never prioritized climate issue.

Also, when it comes to education, of course we are very surprised by the similarity of the problems that we also encounter in our country, especially when it comes to basic education.

During a meeting in Washington a few years ago, a leading Chilean politician, with a career in his government and diplomatic posts abroad said: "everything we have learned and been induced for good reasons to follow, they are now trying to convince us otherwise."

The delay in counting the votes and the archaic system, not only in the party conventions, but also in the system itself, where the delegates choose the president, leave a lot to be desired. The fact that ideological divisions, seen especially in the 2020 vote, and the difficulty of building a constructive dialogue between Democrats and Republicans, calls into question this two-party system, which has practically alternated the command of the country. Also, the two-year term of representatives does not give them enough time to build and support medium- to long-term projects. Politicians who stay in office for a short period of time are basically concerned with not displeasing their voters and managing to stay in Congress. Our multiparty system is at the other extreme, but also difficult to accept, as reality has shown us.

Those supporting Trump argued about his personal relationship with Jair Bolsonaro and that he would be avoiding a socialist regime in the United States, some even talking about communists. However, both arguments seem to be without any basis. In his four-year presidential term, and of all the statements favorable to our country, the bottom line of this Trump–Bolsonaro friendship did not produce many results. As for the argument that Chinese communism would cross borders, it seems to me devoid of any solid rationale with the world. In any case, the fact that Bolsonaro did not immediately acknowledge Biden's victory, waiting for final confirmation after the challenges, I don't think it is relevant for the relationship between the two countries to be weakened.

The polarization in our presidential election in 2022 between Bolsonaro and Lula was very similar to what we have seen in the United States, including an electoral campaign where lies and fake news were widespread.

In the possible dispute with our country, I am convinced that the issue of preserving the Amazon forest will be a fundamental factor, but not a determining one.

I reiterate that the relationship between our countries is far too important and strategic to be dominated by a single issue, however relevant it may be.

Thus, it is fundamental to insist on good relations with the United States, as well as maintaining a relationship with China, Russia, India, Mexico and Argentina, which must be a constant concern of the president and ministers, particularly from Itamaraty.

I reiterate that our problems do not depend on others, but on ourselves, on Brasília, the executive branch, parliament and the different judicial bodies.

In 2022, one of the few countries that Brazil had a deficit in trade accounts was the United States. We imported more from them (there are no strong buyers of commodities).

The international connections and the greater presence of Brazil in the international arena are of the utmost relevance, as I have tried to argue throughout the text, not only through facts, but also through data and testimonials from businessmen and different authorities.

Chapter 7

BRAZIL–CHINA RELATIONS: A NEW ROUTE OF INTERNATIONALIZATION?

The Traditional Partnership

Historically, the relations between Brazil and the United States have always occupied a prominent place in our foreign policy, not only because of our trade and investment relations, but also because of the strong influence of the North American system in the financial and capital markets in a large part of the new Continent, and we are in the Americas.

Our financial institutions, as a rule, were modeled on American ones. The *Comissão de Valores Mobiliários—CVM*, created by Law No. 6385, of 1976, was influenced by the American SEC—Securities and Exchange Commission, created after the Great Depression of 1929.

It is also important not to forget our sociocultural proximity to the North Americans: some knowledge of the English language by a good portion of our society, frequent visits and tourist flows in the great American capitals and cities, not to mention the importance of music and consumption habits, in which American movies have always had an important presence, and also the commercial outlets that have occupied relevant spaces in our cities. We were part, for example, of the Allies in World War II and we had a North American base in Rio Grande do Norte.

Finally, our values and democratic system are very much in line with the American system, and—it is worth remembering—we are part of the same continent.

The New Partnership

In relation to China, however, we have a situation that is still a work in progress. There is a great distance in relation to our customs, admitting that we are very distant from those practiced by Asians, both in terms of form of government, democratic system, religion and language, not to mention the geographical distance between our capitals.

Trade and investment relations between both countries, which did not play an important role before 2008, gained a prominent position recently. As for the tourism, it is limited by the distance factor and the consequent cost of travel, not to mention the difficulties of communication. Only much more recently have we found an increasing number of Chinese business partners with proficiency in English—almost a world language.

This situation changed after 2008, when trade relations with the Chinese expanded substantially and progressively, to the point where China became, in 2009, our most important trade partner. In August 2019, Brazil's trade surplus with China was 33 times higher than with the United States.

China's need to buy agricultural and mineral commodities justified this growing position and, in sequence, was accompanied by investment flows, marking an important position in the area of infrastructure projects, especially in the energy sector, in which it occupies a prominent position, as reported by the Foundation Institute of Administration of the University of São Paulo (USP):

> In the last few years, the sector of generation, transmission, and distribution of electric energy was by far the one that received the most Chinese investments in Brazil.
>
> In 2018 alone, there were 13 confirmed projects in the area.
>
> The big highlights of recent years, however, were initiatives that took place in late 2016 and in 2017.
>
> These are the acquisition of Duke Energy's Brazilian operation by China Three Gorges and of CPFL Energy by State Grid.
>
> As possible future business, there is the interest of Chinese companies in participating in the tender process that will select the company to take over the works of the Angra 3 nuclear power plant.
>
> State Nuclear Power Technology Corporation and China National Nuclear Corporation are two of the Chinese organizations attracted by the opportunity.
>
> Chinese investments in the Brazilian energy sector are so strong that we can say that they are already in a mature phase.[1]

In the first half of 2020, for every dollar Brazil exported to the United States, US$ 3.4 went to China. The trade deficit with the United States was US$3.13 billion, while the trade surplus with China was US$17.65 billion. We imported more from the United States and Argentina together (US$ 16.8 billion) than

---

1 Available at: http://bit.ly/3pFj0U9. Text published on 23 Sept. 2019.

from China (US$ 16.7 billion). China has its fourth largest trade deficit with our country—behind Taiwan, Australia and South Korea.

In a text published by *O Globo*, the consul-general of the Republic of China in Rio de Janeiro, Li Yang, gives a brief account of how the Sino-Brazilian relationship has been developing.

More and more regional aircraft produced in Brazil are flying over the skies of China. Brazil's famous steakhouses come about suddenly. The soft drink Guaraná, the cachaça from Minas Gerais, and brands like Havaianas, Melissa, and Schutz become more accessible to Chinese consumers. Brazilian coffee and propolis are well received. Brazilian soccer players lead their respective Chinese clubs with the ambition to shine brighter. In Brazil, there are several Chinese grocery stores and snack bars scattered in the center of the big cities. DJI—leader in the drone industry—has opened its first physical store in Barra Shopping, in Rio de Janeiro. Cars from Chinese brands such as JAC and Chery have won over Brazilian consumers due to their affordable prices and good service. Rio subway trains were manufactured in China, with air conditioning specially designed for the Brazilian market.

In view of this, it can be seen that Brazil and China have maintained a mutual and beneficial collaboration over time. Over the past 45 years, since the establishment of diplomatic relations between the two countries, cooperation has deepened, and interests are continuously intertwined.

The two countries have signed cooperation agreements in numerous areas, such as aerospace, information technology, biotechnology, agriculture, and livestock, among others. The China-Brazil Earth Resources Satellite Project is recognized as a model of South-South cooperation. Both countries have jointly established the Agricultural Laboratory, the Climate Change and Energy Innovation Technology Center, etc. And currently the construction of the Meteorological Satellite Center and the Biotechnology Center is in process. China has been Brazil's largest trading partner for nine years. In 2017, the trade volume between the two countries reached US$87.54 billion, of which Brazil imported US$28.96 billion and exported US$58.58 billion. The enormous purchasing power of China's 1.4 billion inhabitants is a market that Brazil is in no condition to lose. The Brazilian market has been striving to improve the export structure to China, aiming to sell more high value-added products, rather than *commodities*.

Chinese companies invested $24.7 billion in Brazil in 2017, considered a record in the last seven years. More than 200 of them are based in

Brazil, and many are among the top 500 in the world. In addition, the Brazil-China Cooperation Fund for the Expansion of Productive Capacity, whose total amount is around US$ 20 billion, has already started its operations.[2]

Long-term policy toward China is still to be defined, and it has happened mainly along short-term constraints. One of our interviewees commented: "When we compare ourselves with China, for example, we see a huge difference. They operate thinking in the long term, and we operate in the very short term, when not in short term policies." We miss a state policy to deal with China.

Admittedly, Chinese have a tough way of negotiating that we are registering when we look at trade relations with the United States.

As analyzed by one of our interviewees:

The bilateral relations between Brazil and China have been on an upward curve, a direct result of the strengthening of bilateral relations consolidated over the past 20 years. The enormous thickening of economic relations—especially commercial ones—rests on a solid political trust between the two countries, relations that cannot be seen only as relations between governments, but rather between states.

Brazil is a reliable partner for China, and the Chinese government knows this. We have the ideal conditions to safely supply the main products that China needs, especially in agribusiness. Just by way of contextualization, we should consider that in 2017, Brazil's exports to China reached the value of US$47.49 billion, with an increase of 35.2% compared to 2016.

Bilateral trade—the highest since 2015—reached the value of $74.81 billion in 2017, up 27.9% from the previous year. The Brazil-China trade balance has been positive in the last five years, rising from US$7 billion in 2012 to US$20.2 billion in 2017, recording the highest balance in 2017 (US$27.32 bi) and the lowest result in 2014 (US$3.3 billion).

China was positioned as the 1st destination for Brazilian exports in 2017, with a 21.8% share in the total sales that Brazil made abroad, and also in 1st place as the origin of imports, with 18.1% of the total. More than ever, bilateral relations can be an instrument for our common development.

---

2 Yang, Li. Pathways in China-Brazil cooperation. *O Globo*, 15 Dec. 2019.

We are facing a challenging global scenario, in terms of trade and investment, which reinforces the need for the business community to understand the absolutely strategic role of China in this context. In other words, it is necessary to get to know the country, its respective market, business environment, and investment profile. There is still a long way to go in this area, so that there is an effective complementarity.

It is not about choosing or valuing China over other partners, but rather recognizing that the next decades are likely to be very different from the previous ones, and that China will play a very important role in shaping the new world order.

The so-called asymmetry in the relationship and China's tough negotiating tactics must be recognized. If Trump's American position in the so-called trade dispute is indicative, will it force us to take positions? One of our interviewees summed up this perspective:

So far China, which is our number two export customer, has been complementary to our needs. However, they have a long-term strategy, which we do not have. This in the future could make a—competitive (to express myself contradictorily) cooperation difficult and create difficulties. Investments here are increasing, and ours in China are modest.

We need, with targets, to define a viable strategy, without giving up this important source of investment for the country, particularly for infrastructure. The issue of our lack of planning is always present in the vision of entrepreneurs.

In the interviews we conducted with businessmen and specialists, it was pointed out that competitive segments, such as agribusiness and mining, see China as an opportunity, while noncompetitive sectors find it a threat. The lack of a defined policy toward China extends to other Asian countries as well. Companies like Embraer, which has investments in China, have suffered the same as others with high technological value-added: reduced emphasis on first generation products in order not to suffer the same unfair competition. High-technology intermediate goods companies, such as WEG and Iochpe, have done well to enter the Chinese market and export to global supplier networks.

Small and medium-sized companies, when they can't be more competitive because of imports from China, start partnerships, supplying inputs for Chinese products, which become "Made in China" products with Brazilian components.

A suggestion that we welcome is that SMEs could turn more to prospecting hubs in China. The Foreign Ministry and Apex (Brazilian export promotion), in coordination with business associations, have sought the consolidation or expansion of new markets for products such as coffee, footwear, cars, pork, paper and pulp, and chemicals.

The bargaining power that the Chinese use in the negotiation process due to the size of their market and the crucial issue of knowledge transfer was also present.

It is also worth noting the small number of specialized centers in Brazilian universities dedicated to the Brazil–China relationship.

Finally, in agriculture, where they are our biggest partners, two concerns: extreme dependence on imports from China and the export of raw materials rather than aggregate products.

We also need to expand our presence as part of the BRICSs, because of our great complementarity. The opening of a branch of the BRICS New Development Bank (NDB) in São Paulo is promising. The São Paulo office will be the second regional NDB office worldwide. The headquarters are in Shanghai, China, and the first office was established in 2017 in South Africa. It is also positive that Brazil assumed the presidency of the Bank, in May 2020, through the rotation system, with the election of Marcos Troyjo. He is a diplomat, with extensive knowledge in international relations, from his work at BRIClab, Columbia University, United States and in our foreign policy, as well as special secretary for Foreign Trade and International Affairs at the Ministry of Economy.

Blessing or threat? One contributor mentioned:

> The relationship, as I see it, is ambiguous. Competitive segments—agribusiness, mining, and other segments that competitively exploit natural resources—see China as an opportunity. The non-competitive segments, as a threat. Certainly, our relationship, as revealed by our trade flows, is one of complementarity. Unfortunately, we do not have a defined policy with regard to China and Asia as a whole.

Taking into consideration all that has been registered here about the growing importance of China in bilateral relations and the need for a better and greater understanding on our part, the CEBC—Brazil–China Business Council—launched a study entitled *Bases for a Long Term Strategy of Brazil towards China*,[3] elaborated by Tatiana Rosito, a diplomat experienced in relations with Asian states.

---

3 Available at: http://bit.ly/3ugICu8.

The study focuses on the bilateral relationship between the two countries and proposes improving the relationship around three axes: economy, infrastructure and sustainability.

The Cebri, through its China Analysis Group ("China Group"), has been discussing relevant topics on the Chinese reality and the Brazil–China relationship, aiming to offer bases for an in-depth reflection on the bilateral relationship between the two countries.

Cebri's motivation in creating the China Group was to establish a permanent discussion forum that would continuously and attentively look at the accelerated transformation process of the Chinese scenario, considering its global effects and impacts on Latin America and Brazil, in order to contribute to an analysis of the direction of the bilateral relationship and to define Brazil's strategic positioning vis-à-vis the Asian giant, as well as to help reduce the knowledge deficit about China in Brazilian society.

The China Group is part of Cebri's Asia Center, which is coordinated by Anna Jaguaribe, a counselor of the institution. From its inception in July 2017 until October 2020, the China Group was coordinated by Tatiana Rosito, diplomat and senior fellow at Cebri. As of 2021, the coordination will be passed on to Philip Yang, founder of the Urbem Institute and senior fellow at Cebri.

Between 2017 and the end of 2020, 21 China Group meetings were held, bringing together more than 2,200 participants from Brazil and abroad and producing reports with information for Cebri members and partners as well as the Brazilian government. The meetings were addressed by a total of 77 invited speakers, from different sectors, including academics, government offices, institutional centers and diplomats.

The discussions produced a series of recommendations for Brazil on the directions of the relationship with China, which included:

- Evaluate new opportunities for cooperation and seek further engagement with China;
- Seek a neutral stance in the trade and technology war between the United States and China;
- Approach the Belt and Road Initiative based on dialogue and jointly defined goals;
- Strengthen Brazil's leadership in Latin America's relationship with China, focusing on investment in infrastructure and logistics;
- Establish an instance of effective governmental coordination at the federal level, with a view to broadening the inter-agency dialogue, and with other entities of the Federation and civil society in relation to China;

- Review and update the economic governance instruments, which still reflect an essentially trade-based exchange. It becomes fundamental to have a systemic and longer term strategy regarding China's investments in Brazil that takes into consideration both the externalities of the investments for the productive sector and their technological impact;
- Likewise, to think of trade relations in a more systemic and less short-term manner, with a sectoral vision that encompasses the goods and services chains as a whole and discriminates the export promotion instruments so as to be able to respond to cutting-edge and long-term demands;
- Develop BNDES co-financing mechanism with the CDB (and other Chinese banks);
- Encourage the participation of Asian financial institutions of which Brazil is a part, such as the NDB and the Asian Infrastructure Investment Bank, in addition to other multilateral development banks, in financing sustainable infrastructure in Brazil and explore new financing instruments such as guarantees, syndication and performance bonds;
- Determine a bank responsible for the clearing mechanism of the two national currencies to be operated in Brazil, as regulated by the monetary authorities of the two countries, allowing the direct conversion of Renminbi into Reais and vice-versa;
- Review the bilateral mechanism of the Sino-Brazilian High-Level Commission for Consultation and Coordination (COSBAN) with the objective of making it more agile and maintaining open channels of dialogue with the various agencies of the Chinese government;
- Create a subcommittee on environment and sustainable development within COSBAN;
- Establish a broad partnership in the agri-food area that allows the expansion of exports for items with higher added value in the soybean-animal protein chain (trade and investments, market access, cross-investment, technical cooperation and the establishment of mutually recognized standards in the areas of food health and quality);
- Structure a scientific and industrial collaboration with China in bioeconomics, pharmaceuticals and preventive public health;
- Use the principles of innovation and the digital economy to develop technological infrastructure projects with the aim of increasing the efficiency of productive, financial, trade and service sectors;
- Increase the representativeness of Brazilian companies in China through the creation of representation of the main business associations, with a commercial and investment, intelligence and advocacy role;
- Expand the response and coordination capacity of the Brazilian Embassy in Beijing, including by strengthening coordination in Brazil.

In one of our interviews, an experienced diplomat with a long professional career recorded the following:

> It is impossible to overestimate the importance of China for the Brazilian economy: these are major clients and investors in Brazil. Certainly, Brazilian companies—beyond the agriculture, food and mineral resources sectors, and especially the SMEs—could turn more to prospecting for niches in China. With regard to trade, the MRE and Apex, in strict coordination with the relevant business associations, have sought to promote, by way of market consolidation or opening, sectors such as: coffee, footwear, leather, pork, aircraft, engines and their parts, food, ores, pulp and paper, fuels, and chemicals. Major foreign investors, several Asian companies are interested in the logistics and infrastructure sectors in Brazil, although the appropriate design of frameworks and regulatory-financial structures for this participation is not a trivial task. The Brazilian government, mainly in the framework of the Investment Partnerships Program (PPI), has been giving due treatment to this issue, which also appears frequently, for example, in the work of the instances of the organizational structure of the Brazil-China Cooperation Fund for Expansion of Productive Capacity and in various bilateral cooperation forums. On the other hand, China is a complex country for foreign investment; historically, its attractiveness—due to the size of the market and labor force, disciplined and still relatively low cost inter alia—has given it bargaining power to obtain concessions from foreign investors to associate with Chinese companies and transfer knowledge (including organizational capabilities) and technology, whether or not incorporated into the product.

The relationship with the business community was brought up and discussed a lot by another interviewee:

> In aggregate, it can be said that the business community has a pragmatic relationship with the emergence of China as a global actor, in competition with American power. This emergency is a fait accompli, with both positive and negative developments. For the primary goods exporting sector, the Chinese economy is complementary. For the industrial sector, a vision of competition, predatory to a large extent, prevails. The alignment posture is more prevalent with the medium and small sized companies.

Even if with an extremely pragmatic eye:

Brazilian business must see China as what it really represents for us: the largest and most important customer. But also as a competitor in the Brazilian domestic market for manufactured goods to a lesser degree.

The policy must be *"straight forward."* Treat with the importance that your business' biggest customer deserves. Empathy generated by association with the BRICSs probably helps. Brazil is one of the most complementary countries to China in the world! Brazil benefits from a solid agribusiness and high-quality ore, and China can be a provider of technology/equipment and capital.

As for capital, recent examples are the attempts to participate in deep sea oil drilling tenders and incursions into the Brazilian electrical sector.

Ideological aspects aside, we certainly should not fail to recognize that some of the reflections on Chinese behavior and its possible consequences on the relations between our countries should be considered.

Also in the medium term, many of the products that were exported by China may be replaced by local production, as many countries will want to decrease their degree of dependence on the Asians, even if they eventually have to bear higher costs.

What got even worse in the first four months of 2020 was China's relationship with the United States. President Trump, the Republican Party and many of its leading supporters did not hide their discomfort with the Chinese policy, accusing it of, with WHO support, having delayed the reporting of the new coronavirus, which caused different countries to delay taking the health and hospital measures to organize themselves to face the pandemic.

Each day it became clearer that the China vs. the U.S. relationship transcends the so-called Trade War and is based more on the search for hegemonic power, in a long process whose unfoldings will certainly affect us. The U.S. presidential elections in November 2020, and the return to power of a Democratic President, make us think that perhaps relations will be guided by less aggression and more dialogue, although without radical changes at the core.

On 15 July 2020, the *New York Times* indicated that the two countries were going through the worst time in their relationship. Technological, military and territorial disputes (Hong Kong, for example) rage between the two powers and point to the emergence of a new geopolitical order, turbocharged by ideological differences and the Covid-19 pandemic, which affected the United States violently. Although the United States often advocates economic separation by abruptly cutting off the use of Chinese products for U.S. companies, this does not seem to be a realistic policy in the short term, and even in the medium to long term it is a high-cost policy for Americans, as indicated elsewhere in the text.

On a positive note, in the Bali summit Biden and Xi Jinping met for the second time face-to-face, and both agreed to establish limits on their disputes in order to avoid a war.

China is a sphinx: "Decipher me or I will devour you!". The relationship between the two great powers is no longer a commercial dispute but a struggle for hegemony in a fragmented world.

The U.S. presidential elections in November 2020, with a Democratic president returning to power, did not bring radical change regarding China. Nor does the Democratic Party harbor a differentiated position from the Republican Party, largely reflecting American public opinion, which is not sympathetic to the Chinese.

In the world of international trade, after years of very difficult negotiations, China and 14 other countries signed a Pacific region trade agreement, coordinated by Beijing, on 14 November 2020.

The "Regional Comprehensive Economic Partnership" (RCEP) involves about one-third of the world's GDP. The main goal is to strengthen free trade, which, in the signatories' opinion, is of the utmost relevance, particularly after the pandemic that made countries look more inward. In terms of the global economy, it is already considered the world's largest free trade agreement. The countries include some of the most dynamic economies on the globe and also nations with recent bilateral trade tensions, such as China and Australia.

The United States is not part of the agreement, having its efforts involved in the Trans-Pacific Partnership, launched by Barack Obama, which did not include China, and was seen as an attempt to contain Beijing. However, with Donald Trump's administration, the rejection of multilateralism has led to the failure of that initiative.

RCEP now puts pressure on Biden's administration to act on an area of influence from China. "Encouraging free trade is even more important now that the global economy is slumping and there are signs that countries are turning inward," argued Japan's prime minister Yoshihide Suga during a meeting with the other RCEP leaders, according to government officials.

An important point to be highlighted is the incentive to labor mobility. Although there is no free transit of people, the countries will facilitate multiple recognition of diplomas.

The countries that have signed the agreement are Brunei, Cambodia, Indonesia, Laos, Malaysia, Myanmar, Philippines, Singapore, Thailand, Vietnam, Australia, China, Japan, South Korea and New Zealand.

According to the Japanese government, the RCEP will eliminate tariffs on goods traded between members, further reducing trade barriers with many of Japan's major partners.

The agreement still needs to be ratified by the national governments. It is worth remembering that it has been eight years of negotiations and that India, which was part of the initial negotiations, in 2019 pulled out of the agreement for fear that it would lead to a flood of imports, affecting local producers.

In any case, it does not seem to us that the RCEP, from the point of view of trade between Asian countries, would have to strengthen, to impact international trade between countries that are not integrated into it.

Another variable that may have relevance is a proposal that emerged at the end of November and was covered by the London *Financial Times*. The European Union has come to propose to the United States to create a new global alliance. The preliminary plan would propose to revitalize the partnership with the United States in various areas, from digital regulation, management of the pandemic caused by Covid-19, to fighting deforestation. The Europeans argue that the EU–U.S. partnership needs maintenance and renewal for the democratic world to assert its interest from what they call "potential autocracies" and "closed economies" that counter exploit the openness our societies depend on.

The plan presented supports the idea of President-elect Joe Biden holding a summit meeting of the democracies, and that the bilateral agenda should have as its "foundation to create a new world alliance of like-minded countries." The war in Ukraine strengthened the ties between the United States and EU.

It is worth nothing that there is a 19-page document that was to be presented at a meeting for national endorsement on December 2020: "as democratic societies and open market economies, the EU and the US agree about the strategic challenges posed by China's growing international assertiveness, although they do not always agree on how best to tackle the issue." The cards are on the table.

I think this EU initiative is still unclear as to whether it will achieve the desired objectives, but it does show that as Chinese diplomacy has become more aggressive, it has aroused reactions not only in the United States, but also in some of the large EU countries. It remains to be seen to what extent there will be unity and whether the European countries will agree to a more comprehensive confrontation. Many doubts have already arisen in this regard.

In October 2022, the Communist Party elected Xi Jinping for a third term as the supreme head of state of China. Reactions were mixed, but the prevailing view was that giving Xi almost dictatorial power was not a positive for China and relations with the Western world.

Leading economic experts project that the economic golden era is gone. The policy of trying to eliminate Covid-19 from Chinese territory at any cost proved to be more troublesome than initially expected. Successive lockdowns in their most important cities, responsible for goods production and external trade, were a factor affecting their GDP growth rate and also for the world economy. Growth estimated for 2022 was lower than 3 percent, the same for 2023.

In late 2022, under pressure from widespread protests, Beijing was compelled to reconsider their draconian Covid-19 quarantine policy. The price of this relaxation in terms of human lives lost remains to be seen.

Chapter 8

SPECIAL CONTRIBUTION: FROM INDIFFERENCE TO FEAR?

The history of our foreign policy, marked by competent Itamaraty actions in a line originating with the Baron of Rio Branco, has been losing its importance since the Dilma government and, today, has reached international insignificance under former foreign minister Ernesto Araújo.

We have lost the direction of a policy of multilateralism and the capacity to be mediators in our own region, of which we are natural leaders. Leadership that we gave up when, under Lula's government, we uncritically joined the group of leftist countries in Latin America and to mark our presence in the world through ideological positions, rather than through our state interests.

There were times when Brazilian interests were above ideologies. Even during the military dictatorship, our foreign policy was able to resume diplomatic relations with Mao Zedong's China and to recognize the former Portuguese colonies as independent, despite their ties to Portugal and the actions of communist groups in liberation.

Unlike the Lula administration, when a South–South policy was established, which minimized the relationship with the United States, then our main economic partner, now, under the Bolsonaro government, a fond relationship has been formed with the United States in which its importance is maximized to the detriment of countries governed by different ideologies than those of the current government, such as Argentina or China, today our main economic partner.

Brazil has always sought to base its foreign policy on pacifism, on the ability to border 10 countries without any serious problems over the years, on natural leadership in South America. Because of its size, its internal market, its geopolitical situation, its potentially powerful economy, still among the 10 largest in the world, Brazil has qualified to be an important partner in the globalized world.

However, the spirit of the positions we have expressed throughout our history has been lost over time, and today we are no longer part of the group of countries through which the great issues of the globalized world pass: environment, human rights, the Middle East.

Historically, we have always aspired to a more influential role in international organizations. We have had some victories, such as with Ambassador Roberto Azevêdo as President of the WTO, but also several diplomatic failures. The biggest, to date, is the nonmembership in the UN Security Council, a claim that comes since the end of World War II, in which Brazil was the only Latin American country to participate alongside the Allies.

After World War II, President Roosevelt recommended that Brazil be considered as a possible sixth member of the Security Council, but there was resistance from the Soviet Union and England. Brazil had already had a negative experience at the Hague Conference, between the end of the nineteenth and beginning of the twentieth century, when the European powers defined that some nations, for reasons of power, should have more influence on the decision-making process than others.

But there are positive experiences to note. It is true that today we are part of the BRICS, the union of Brazil, Russia, India, China and South Africa, and also of the G20, a group that gathers the 20 most influential nations and that, in this world interconnected by technology, has been an extended forum of the G7.

Brazil's role was once central in international environmental policy, a cornerstone of Western society, an importance that we gradually lost as the issue ceased to be a priority for our government, when it came into conflict with the main international organizations and environmental associations, disconnecting itself from contemporary public policies.

Disconnecting from modernity, by the way, is characteristic of Brazilian governments, which have already made market reserve to protect the nascent technological industry, generating distancing from the great international production chains, with subsidies to industries, which, as a result, lost their competitiveness in an increasingly interconnected and globalized world. We have islands of excellence that only confirm the rule.

Like every radical experience such as the one we lived through in the Covid-19 pandemic, this one will also provoke perceptible changes in the outlook of humanity, from the revaluation of interpersonal relations after months in quarantine, to the rearrangement of international geopolitics, with the main players reviewing positions and seeking to overcome deficiencies that were exposed, some surprising, as the dependence of the West, even the United States, on health care equipment and medicines that are mostly man-ufactured in China. The local production of strategic products, and not only health products, has become a priority in the planning of the main nations.

Financial and economic globalization, which has led to the paroxysm of Western capitalism taking advantage of the absence of labor protection policies and human rights of a dictatorship like China, and other Asian countries to increase their profits, will certainly lead to the new geopolitical view, and capitalism will inevitably have to turn to social protection of citizens in order to survive in a world where income inequality has been obscenely exposed, and other defects have resurfaced, such as selfishness, racism and xenophobia. Covid-19 came to remind us of the fragility of the human being and to emphasize the dependence that each one has on the other.

The environment, which had already gained an importance that only the deranged would not admit, now that the world has stopped for months, its essentiality to the planet became explicit and the clarity that the pollution produced by savage capitalism reduces the possibility of existence of the human species.

In this new international framework, Brazil has become a pariah among Western nations. A country that, due to neglect and negligence of an insane government, has placed itself in the top of the ranking of the most affected by the pandemic, with the risk of being one of the most infected and deadliest countries on the planet, leads to the borders being closed to its people and its products, already hit by the terrible reputation of the government's environmental policies. Is Brazil afraid of the world? Or is the world now afraid of Brazil?

by *Merval Pereira*[1]

---

1 Journalist and writer, member of the Brazilian Academy of Letters. He is a columnist for *O Globo*.

Part 3

BORDERLESS INVESTMENTS

Chapter 9

INVESTMENTS IN CAPITAL MARKETS ABROAD

When we analyze the inhibiting factors to a more active and consistent participation of Brazilian companies abroad, which has fluctuated depending on cyclical aspects, the same cannot be said about the investments of individuals abroad.

It would be perfectly explainable that those who have accumulated a certain level of wealth (accumulated savings) would seek diversification to compose their portfolio looking for opportunities that exist in other stock markets, fixed income, bonds, different types of funds, etc. around the globe.

This flow of resources had a greater acceleration due to the behavior of different variables of the Brazilian economy and also due to the political scenario. I remember that, when the discussion of the reform of the Constitution was being held, there was fear of the ways in which we were being led and how market economy values would be revised.

Without exhausting the subject here, I would draw attention to some of the aspects that can most influence these investments abroad:

- *Exchange rates*, especially the dollar, have always been an important referential, and when our currency was at different times overvalued, more favorable conditions were created for investing abroad;
- Overvalued *local assets* or little confidence in the projected returns of listed companies;
- Attractive *interest rates* abroad, considering the type of risk involved in comparative terms. The substantial drop in the interest rate, which by the end of 2020 was around 2 percent, with inflation by the National Broad Consumer Price Index (IPCA) being at 3.5 percent, led many investors to invest abroad, in search of better results.
- *Political risk* is an obvious factor for investment allocation. Many investors, at different moments of the troubled local political scene, prevailing in much of the past, have felt more comfortable in allocating part of their

resources abroad. Distrust in our currency and also, at times, in our institutions;

- *Predictability*: Alteration of preestablished policies and regulations, compromising previously made decisions. Foreign investors are very concerned about constantly changing rules;

- *Globalization* brings the factor that markets are becoming global and that information between different markets is circulating in real time, thus greatly stimulating the flow of capital. Also, liquidity and facilities are a factor;

- *Legislation*: Looking through the rearview mirror, when I started at Deltec (1958), it was rare for financial intermediaries to have transparent structures for investing domestic investors' savings abroad. It was not encouraged, and to some extent frowned upon, for anyone to invest abroad through the "parallel" market. Brazilian investors were not allowed to invest abroad and were not granted formal registration by the monetary authority.

I remember well that when Deltec offered in Brazil an investment fund for investments abroad (*Fond d'Investissement pour l'Amérique Latine*), their local advisors reacted very negatively and boycotted the initiative. At that time it was not "politically correct" to invest abroad. Quite indicative of how Brazilians viewed investing abroad: a crime against the country!

When BACEN (Banco Central do Brasil) regulated the operations for investments abroad, which no longer became "off the books," this flow of resources was gradually expanded, not only by this faculty, as well as the fact that a large number of financial intermediaries were already established in the country, particularly banks from the United States and European countries. Not to mention the "financial boutiques," which also started to offer their services to investors to diversify their investments abroad. Therefore, the globalized market offered opportunities to all those who were willing to take risks outside our borders. Private banking also started to have an impact advising those who wanted to invest abroad.

The figures on the investments of Brazilians abroad today are available from the Central Bank, with additional information. After all, all those who have registered resources are required to fill out the Declaration of Brazilian Capitals Abroad annually.

Institutional investors (mainly from pension funds) were initially not allowed to invest part of their assets abroad. However, the resolution of the National Monetary Council (CMN) No. 3792, of September 2009, allowed that up to 10 percent of these resources could be directed to foreign investments. Despite this possibility, according to data available from the Association of Pension

Funds, these investments are not yet relevant in the percentage of their assets but have good growth potential.

The Covid-19 factor and the large depreciation of the Brazilian real in the first half of 2020 created serious doubts about the attractiveness of investing abroad. Also, another factor was the loss of value of assets in Brazil and the price attractiveness, as several analysts pointed out. But despite a less favorable exchange rate, still, in the first semester, investments abroad increased.

Those who invest abroad take into consideration the desirable liquidity and the need for diversification between the domestic and foreign markets. Obviously, the exchange rate plays an important role in this foreign allocation and in the analysis between local and foreign opportunities. Obviously, the trust factor is fundamental to decide the allocation, whether here or abroad.

Chapter 10

FOREIGN CAPITAL IN THE LOCAL MARKET

Since my first professional days in an investment bank, I have been involved in the activity of seeking foreign investment for our capital markets. Regardless of the period we lived through, we have always had a strong motivation to seek external savings. Foreign investors in the stock market or in debt securities would not only increase the level of savings, which here would be added to the existing savings by local investors, as it would be beneficial in increasing opportunities for companies that consider looking to the market as a source of long-term financing.

Initially, and I speak here of the late 1950s, when I started working as an analyst at Deltec Investments, Credit and Financing, a company created by Wall Street salesmen, there was a need to educate the investing public. It was to sell Brazil as a good place to invest and, as a consequence, to point out the existing opportunities for those who were willing to diversify their resources in a market that had not yet been explored. Multiples of the stocks traded in our market were low when compared to their peers abroad. At that time, the nomenclature of an "emerging country" did not yet exist and would only appear later.

At that point there was no specific legislation to facilitate the investor in the stock market and in investment funds. As far as I remember, the regulatory procedures of the old Superintendence of Money and Credit (Sumoc), or later, when the Bacen was created in 1965, were almost the same, whether the investor was acquiring control or a relevant stake in a Brazilian corporation, or, alternatively, whether he was acquiring a few shares of Belgo Mineira, Brahma or Villares, leading corporations in the stock exchange.

The concern of the monetary authorities lay in the flow of funds—whether it would be possible to schedule the matching outflow, when receiving the inflow. When someone invested in stocks, they didn't know when, and how much, would flow out. *Cash flow* was a factor for monetary authorities.

There was also a nationalistic component—the fear of denationalization of corporations via the purchase of bearer shares. I remember well that during my mandate as the first president of the CVM, we insisted a lot with the Central Bank on the flexibility of Decree-Law No. 1401, of 1975, so that there would be a mechanism that would give some flexibility compared to the referred legislation. The scheme was very complex and discouraging! For example, the investor could not buy stocks directly, but through a specially created investment fund, and that it would have to be managed (or co-administered) through a local institution (investment bank), who was responsible to the local financial authorities.

At that time, the level of interest of potential investors was higher, and some national institutions had the basic function of disseminating information about listed companies and existing opportunities.

We received frequent visits from some institutions that wanted to better understand the market potential. Banco de Investimento do Brasil (BIB), an association of Deltec and Banco Moreira Salles, was one of the first to seek investments abroad as soon as the legislation was passed. We wanted to evaluate the interest of foreign institutions in the new regulation, especially those that had already shown interest in the possibility of investing here. European institutional investors were the most present, and U.S. institutional investors were practically absent. It was for example the case of Robeco from the Netherlands (one of Europe's largest fund managers) who decided to invest US$15 million in a fund named Robrasco, a mutual fund managed by Unibanco Investment Bank.

One of the pioneering country funds created by U.S. investors was the *Brazil Fund*, launched by *First Boston Corporation* and liquidated in 2005. It was the first vehicle designed to receive funds from foreign investors in the market with a public offering by Merrill Lynch. Being a corporation, they elected a board of which some distinguished Brazilians were part. It was a successful story and is detailed in my book *Capital Markets: Past, Present and Future*,[1] reproduced below:

> The market was inaccessible. Brazil and other developing countries in the region had a virtually closed economy. Very few invested abroad, and the reverse was also true. Only in the 1970s did the market begin to open up. Just to give you an idea, in 1976, when Brazil opened the stock exchange to foreign investment, supported by Decree-Law 1,401/1975, I traveled to Europe, as vice president of Banco de Investimentos do

---

1 *Valeu a Pena! Mercado de Capitais: Passado, Presente e Futuro.* São Paulo, 2018.

Brasil (BIB), to offer investments in the Brazilian stock exchange. The process that was approved by the authorities was complex and bureaucratic, not allowing direct investments in stocks, but through an investment fund specially created for this purpose.

I could see that some countries, including France, did not allow individuals to invest abroad, and only corporations and institutions were allowed after prior consultation with the Bank of France.

The same was true in Germany and Italy. The most receptive investors, from the point of view of overseas investments, were in the UK. North American investors and funds did not show interest in our market, so much so that they did not form the basis of the first investment funds created in Brazil. Edinburgh, for example, was the mecca for large investment funds with a tradition of interest in investing their funds in other markets. They have always been important investors abroad, with some pioneering investment in emerging markets. The Rotterdamsch Beleggings Consortium (Robeco) fund from the Netherlands was the pioneer to take an interest in the Brazilian market and gave BIB the management for many years of the Robrasco fund, specially created to receive their resources, until runaway inflation discouraged them to stay in the country.

I was on a preparatory trip abroad about the interest of foreigners in the market when the legislation (Decree Law No. 1,401) was sanctioned. It was quite complex, because among other things, it did not allow foreign investors to invest directly in listed companies. It would be through an investment fund specially created for this purpose and managed by domestic financial institutions, management contract, etc. There were different types of contracts, regulating the relationship between investor and manager, custody, etc.

In London, I was informed that the legislation had finally been enacted, with the complexities indicated. With the help of a former secretary, who coincidentally worked in our London consulate, we prepared all the documentation, adapting it to Robeco (and that required hours of work at the Savoy Hotel) to go to Netherlands and present it to the managers of the company. Mr. Brower, managing director, was very receptive and, to make my life easier, was willing to meet me at the Amsterdam Schiphol airport to discuss the possible application.

We ended up creating the specialized fund (Robrasco), in which we formed a board of directors in which they were present, as well as a representative from Phillips, and Arie de Geus from Royal Dutch Shell, who helped us a lot with the alternative scenarios approach to strategic planning, which he pioneered.

The most effective process of internationalization of the Brazilian market started at the end of the 1980's, the initial milestone being the enactment of CMN Resolution 1,289/1987 and its annexes. Starting in the 1990s, the country's economy showed signs of acceleration, opening up to the foreign market and allowing foreign investors to operate in the national territory.

The Brazil Fund was organized with the support of the Brazilian government as part of the effort to open up our capital market to foreign investors. It was the first vehicle designed to invest in Brazilian stocks, registered for a public offering in the United States.

It began operations in April 1988, following an offering of 12 million shares sold at $12.50 each. The First Boston Corporation has been selected by the Brazilian government as one of the leading underwriters in the campaign along Merrill Lynch Inc's capital markets division. The Brazil Fund was a closed-end investment fund and had its shares traded at NYSE.

Initially, I was part of its advisory board, together with Carlos Moacyr Gomes de Almeida, Geraldo Hess, Julien Chacel, and Otto Bohn. Later, I joined its board of directors, along with Ronaldo Nogueira, my university classmate and a long-time capital market professional, who created IMF Editora. Today, his son, Ronnie Nogueira, edits the successful magazine *Revista RI—Relações com Investidores*.

In 2005, its shareholders opted to liquidate the fund, distributing its assets net to the shareholders.

Globalization, or internationalization as some prefer, is twofold. The first is that some attitudes that were tolerable in a closed market— in which the rules of the game were settled, because it was a kind of closed club—have changed, which is obviously positive. These are new standards of behavior and new rules to which the market agents must submit. The question of corporate governance, for example, is an adaptation of concepts adopted in other countries and is being continuously assimilated. To compete, markets must have a determined governance in raising resources.

Another aspect in markets is linked to the fact that we effectively have two levels of actors. On one side, those who really act and are subject to the rules of the game, because they already have a size that forces them to adopt adequate practices, with policies compatible with the rules of globalization. On the other hand, there are those who continue to operate in local markets, without access to global markets and who therefore do not feel bound by more stringent rules of conduct. In time, they will become marginalized unless they adjust to the new demands.

Episodes in the last five years show that companies that started to have shares traded in the foreign market (particularly the USA) must be subject to the regulations of these markets, mainly the SEC and the Department of Justice (DOJ).

In 1983 the Organization of Securities Commissions (IOSCO) was created, bringing together securities commissions from all over the world, with the objective of an exchange of ideas and experiences about their respective markets. The CVM was one of the founders of this initiative, and one of the first meetings was held in Brazil, prior to the formal creation of IOSCO.

With the objective of seeking the convergence of accounting standards, in 2001 the International Accounting Standards Board— IASB, whose objectives were outlined at its foundation by its trustees, led by Paul Volcker. IASB has been working to propose standards suitable for universal acceptance and increase the usefulness and credibility of the financial statements of companies that issue securities in different international markets.

I was part of its first board of trustees as the Latin America representative, where I developed a good relationship with Paul Volcker, former President of the Federal Reserve Bank of USA (1979-1987).

These efforts were aimed at adopting standards of excellence in the measurement and disclosure of assets, liabilities, equity, and results, as a precondition for stronger and more efficient capital markets that will contribute to well-capitalized companies and more and more able to generate wealth and jobs.

In addition, the framework for global accounting standards is already in place in much of the world. Within the G20, 3/4 of the countries will be making domestic use of IFRS standards.

Even if the US did not allow the domestic use of IFRS standards, US investors have invested more than $7 trillion at that time, in companies using IFRS standards. Many US companies have subsidiaries that will produce IFRS-compliant reports/balance sheets, while about 500 foreign companies listed on the American markets use these standards.

For these reasons, IASB is committed to keeping the IFRS standards as convergent as possible to US Gaap. IASB says that if the Financial Accounting Standards Board (Fasb) brings good ideas before it, then it will steal them as quickly as possible. They claim to have no shame in such an attitude, and good accounting ideas cannot be patented!

This is the case with corporate governance in Europe. In the USA Canada and Great Britain, where most publicly traded companies have dispersed ownership, the core of corporate governance is relevant. In continental Europe and Latin America, where the figure of the controlling shareholder predominates, the priority of corporate governance is to protect minority shareholders from the controlling shareholder. It should be remembered that we have seen many cases of abuse of minorities.

The original legislation was modified at the end of the 1980s, with CMN Resolution No. 1289/1987. Ary Oswaldo Mattos Filho, who presided over the CVM from 1990 to 1992, managed to make the rules for investing in the stock market and in investment funds more flexible, which opened new horizons for the market.

When the stock market went through a crisis between 1971 and 1975, considered one of the deepest crises in our market., Mário Henrique Simonsen, who was finance minister in Ernesto Geisel government, came to the conclusion that capital markets needed greater external participation and higher inclusion of foreign participants.

Simultaneously, the corporate legislation was revised, and the Securities and Exchange Commission of Brazil (CVM) was created as mechanisms to recreate the market. Now, institutions settled in the country through the banks that represented them and started to produce corporate analyses about securities market, with more disclosure, including quarterly data.

I remember that in 1961, Deltec launched the Deltec Index, which tracked the behavior of the stocks of the main companies with shares traded on the stock exchange. It was a pioneer in launching a study with the retrospective of companies traded on the stock exchange, comparatively over the last five years, and the price–earnings ratio in the stock exchange listing.

However, at that time, foreign investors always had a negative bias toward buying Brazilian stocks, because, as a rule, they were investing in preferred stock, without voting rights (that would only exist if it did not pay a priority dividend after three years). And there was the distrust in our currency because of persistent high inflation.

The Brazilian legislation allowed up to two-thirds of the company's capital not to have voting rights. Another limiting factor was poor corporate governance, which was not up to date with the standards practiced in more developed markets. With the recommendations, mainly from foreign investors, there was an important improvement in the legislation in a progressive way.

This situation has changed, not only with the increased presence of institutional investors in the market, which has demanded greater quantity and quality of information, but also with the expansion of minority shareholder rights. There were complaints that Brazilian listed companies did not practice equitable policies between stakeholders and shareholders.

Right now, a growing number of Brazilian corporations, most of them listed in the market, are adopting ESG (environmental, social and corporate governance) concept to reach sustainable development goals.

Obviously, the desire was to have the governance rules prevailing in their country of origin here, so as to minimize their risks. The creation of the Novo Mercado (NM) by the São Paulo Stock Exchange, in 2000, came, in part, to fulfill this desire, creating a special status for companies that adhered to this differentiated segment, assuring them, in the launching of Level 1 shares, the right to vote. Therefore, that set of companies would eventually integrate this new segment, starting in the year 2000. Particularly between 2004 and 2005, a considerable number of companies that went public, through so-called Initial Public Offerings, did so by launching common shares and later observing ESG guidelines.

Of the companies that went to market during this period, a predominant portion of the offerings ended up being underwritten by foreign investors. But not only in the primary market does the presence of foreign investors stand out. They also had a strong presence in the stock exchange, and the statistics revealed with great frequency by the Bacen and the B3 (São Paulo Stock Exchange) show the increase or decrease of their presence.

One of the initiatives of the NM was the creation of the Câmara de Arbitragem do Mercado (CAM), of the then BVSP, and which was intended to be the venue for any shareholder disputes between NM member companies. I have been the president of the CAM since its creation in 2001 to the present day.

In a country with limited savings, such as Brazil, and with an important need for capital for growth, the participation of foreign capital is of fundamental relevance. For this, predictability and respect for the rules of the game and market economy are predominant factors in attracting foreign capital. As always, the educational factor must be present, making it clear for investors the need to combat insider trading, which I believe is a strong negative.

The 32 percent devaluation of the real (between 31 December 2019 and 30 November 2020), as well as in other periods, could be one of the factors in attracting foreign capital, there being confidence in the institutions and in overcoming the new coronavirus crisis and the serious political situation, which generated additional uncertainties. The binomial of trust and predictability must always to be present.

A positive sign, even considering risks with the rise in stock prices and without considering the possible drop in profitability of companies due to the effects of the pandemic, the number of individuals who started to invest in the stock markets has increased substantially.

In 2020, public offerings approached R$ 120 billion, compared to R$ 89.6 billion in 2019, with a tendency for the first quarter of 2021 to hold steady.

The crises created by Covid-19, and most recently with the war in Ukraine, affected most stock markets around the world. Our market and stock markets were seen by some investors as a safe haven in a turbulent world, particularly in the second semester of 2022. Our losses were lower than developed markets.

Chapter 11

SPECIAL CONTRIBUTION: DOM CABRAL FOUNDATION HAS THE FLOOR[1]

Fundação Dom Cabral has been closely following the internationalization movement of Brazilian companies for many years. And it found that the advance of the participation of these companies in the studies,[2] as well as the degree of internationalization, has evolved gradually over the years:

- 2006: 24 companies with an average internationalization index of 12.9 percent;
- 2020–21: 154 companies with an average internationalization rate of 20.7 percent, that is, a growth of 62.3 percent in 16 years.

Throughout the 15 editions, Brazilian companies have gradually increased their internationalization index (an increase of approximately 1 percentage point each year), which shows a slow but growing insertion in international markets.

The most recent editions of the study,[3] released in 2020 and 2021, bring together historical analyses of more than 150 large and medium-sized companies that have gone through the survey and which, in some cases, are highly internationalized. Some examples of participating companies, with national relevance, that stood out in their internationalization strategies were: Embraer, Stefanini, WEG, Marcopolo, Fitesa, Iochpe-Maxion, Metalfrio,

---

1 Chapter written in partnership with the Fundação Dom Cabral. Special thanks to Lívia Barakat, Viviane Barreto de Azevedo Lamego and Antonio Batista.

2 *Trajetórias FDC de Internacionalização das Empresas Brasileiras, Ranking FDC das Multinacionais Brasileiras* and *Ranking FDC das Transnacionais Brasileiras* are the studies that FDC has been conducting since 2006.

3 *Trajetórias FDC de Internacionalização das Empresas Brasileiras*—Special Edition and Edition 2021.

Gerdau, Tigre, Localiza, Randon, CI&T, Alpargatas, JBS, Marfrig, Vale, Odebrecht, Intercement, Braskem, DMS among others. Together, these multinationals are present in 89 countries on every continent in the world except Antarctica.

In 2020,[4] when asked about their plans for the next two years in the markets in which they were already active, 67.0 percent of the companies participating in the survey planned major expansion, while 19.0 percent planned to keep activities stable in those markets, and only 3.0 percent intended to retrench their operations. Furthermore, 70.7 percent planned to enter new countries in the next two years, indicating that the internationalization movement of Brazilian companies should continue to grow.

Between 2016 and 2020,[5] the top 10 countries with the presence of own subsidiaries and/or franchises of participating companies were the United States (53 companies), Argentina (38 companies), Mexico (29 companies), Colombia (28 companies), Chile (27 companies), Uruguay (25 companies), Peru (24 companies), China (21 companies), United Kingdom (20 companies) and Paraguay (18 companies). Therefore, a strong predilection of the participants in the markets of the Americas can be seen, especially to the first destination of its subsidiaries or franchises, which is related to geographical and cultural proximity. Between 2011 and 2018, Colombia was the country that received most Brazilian companies (16 companies), followed by China and Peru (13 companies each). In FDC's studies, as expected, China appears as an important trade partner for Brazil. Of the 55 companies that operate abroad through their own subsidiaries, China is their main destination outside the Americas.[6] The special edition also shows that Asia is one of the regions that had the least evasion of Brazilian companies in the period from 2011 to 2018, possibly due to the greater insertion in global value chains and access to lower cost inputs. When the medium-sized companies are analyzed, 73 percent do not operate physically in other countries, and 21 percent operate with commercial representatives to support exports.[7]

Furthermore, the most recent edition has shown an expansion of startup companies and their respective contribution to the internationalization process. A total of 26 companies were identified as startups and they showed that their speed to internationalize was three times faster than traditional firms, with an average of 6.2 years to establish the first international subsidiary

---

4 *Trajetórias de Internacionalização das Empresas Brasileiras* 2018.
5 *Trajetórias FDC de Internacionalização das Empresas Brasileiras*—Special Edition.
6 *Trajetórias de Internacionalização das Empresas Brasileiras* 2018.
7 *Internationalization of Medium-Sized Enterprises*—FDC, 2019.

abroad against the average of 19.5 years of traditional firms. These companies have also shown more interest to enter new markets through R&D, which demonstrates their propensity to innovate.

With the Covid-19 crisis, internationalization movements have fallen off and we have observed a greater tendency to concentrate operations in the domestic market, not only in Brazil, but worldwide. The United Nations Conference on Trade and Development (UNCTAD)[8] estimates that FDI flows are expected to fall between 30 and 40 percent in 2020–21. The crisis will also strongly affect the financial result of the 5,000 largest multinationals in the world, which are expected to see a 30 percent drop in revenues by 2020, according to UNCTAD.

A report by fDi Intelligence[9] shows that Brazil was the world's fourth leading destination for capital investments in 2019, having shown 103 percent growth over the previous year. However, this trend was also deeply affected by the Covid-19 crisis. According to the Central Bank, in the month of April 2020, net inflows in country direct investments totaled US$234 million, down from US$5.1 billion in April 2019, a 95.4 percent drop in one year. Also, according to the Central Bank, Brazilian direct investments abroad have also shown a decline since the beginning of the Covid-19 crisis. In April 2020, net FDI flows showed disinvestments of about US$ 4.8 billion. When asked if the internationalization strategy of the company has been affected by the context of Covid-19, 24.0 percent of the respondents stated that their strategy was somehow affected, and 21.0 percent answered that it was impacted by the global social–political–economic context.

Fundação Dom Cabral warns that companies must develop competencies to plan, evaluate and rethink their internationalization process in order to take better advantage of the opportunities that may arise from the global market. The digital transformation, which has already been happening and gaining space in companies all over the world, shows itself as an ally for international performance in times of global recession and great local concentration of investments. Different business models facilitated by new technologies represent interesting alternatives to enable the global insertion of Brazilian companies. For example, e-commerce facilitates sales abroad and could greatly support exports, which should become more relevant with the devaluation of the real. Technologies such as 3-D printers and AI can come associated with production systems in other countries in partnership with local companies, with little or no need for technical and managerial staff

---

8 Available at: http://bit.ly/3aAq8gz.
9 Available at: https://bit.ly/2ZttNX0.

coming from Brazil. The advance of communication technologies and greater flexibility in work models, driven by the rapid transition to home office, will also give more flexibility for managing multilocation teams and reduce the need for expatriations and recurrent business travel. All this has shown that it is possible to act globally, relying on strategic partnerships, more frequent communications and greater trust in local teams. International business diversification can reduce the risks of overdependence on the domestic market and provide access to markets that recover more quickly.

Times of great uncertainty lead people to seek security. Even with the various paradoxes present in the global scenario, trust is an increasingly important asset. Never has technology been used so much and people are becoming more and more fundamental. Technology is a means to support the implementation of strategies created by people. In a report dated 16 May 2020, with the title "Returning to work in the future of work—Embracing purpose, potential, perspective and possibility during Covid-19," Deloitte invites organizations to reexamine whether there really is a conflict between technology and the human, and how it is possible to address an apparent paradox and find ways to remain human in a technology-driven world.

The collective virtual environment has raised the need for leaders to prepare themselves to command in this "new normal" and to engage their teams in remote work. The moment demands taking care of people and making them open-minded to take advantage of the opportunities that the crisis can bring to the business. The word crisis in Chinese is composed of two ideograms, one meaning danger, the other opportunity. The starting point is to be prepared to be able to differentiate one thing from another.

As far as the Fundação Dom Cabral sector is concerned, of executive education, we observe a strong impact of the current context. Research conducted by Unicon Consortium for University-Based Executive Education of 14 April 2020, with business schools from all continents, on Covid-19's Impacts on Executive Education, shows that larger schools expect a larger decline in enrollment than smaller ones. On the expected financial impact of business schools in fiscal year 2020, the consolidated survey shows that 37 percent of schools estimate a drop in revenues between 31 and 40 percent, and 34 percent of schools estimate a drop of more than 40 percent in revenues.

CNN Business published a story on 22 April 2020, titled "She paid $68,000 to do an MBA at Cambridge. Now she's studying via Zoom in India," where it relates the frustration of Srishti Warman who dreamed for so many years of taking her MBA at the Judge Business School at Cambridge University and, after starting the course in September 2019, could not imagine that six months later she would be in India finishing her course in the on-line mode, direct from her parents' home in Chandigarh, a city north of Delhi.

Overall, in March 2020, schools needed to transform face-to-face deliveries into on-line mode in one weekend. This action, perhaps, is the smallest part of the transformation. There are bigger challenges, for example: How to demonstrate the school's value proposition in the digital learning environment? Schools will need to adapt to a new reality that is here to stay. Mobility restrictions and health standards should make schools adapt their value proposition to the digital medium, considering the blended mode (on-site + on-line).

The most important change, according to Dan LeClair, president of the Global Business School Network, is innovations to support peer-to-peer learning, that is: How to make MBA students or participants of an organizational development program feel part of teams and learn from each other in this new context? Networking *is* an important part of the value proposition. It is important to emphasize the importance of the exchange of experiences between the students/participants, which goes beyond the transmission of knowledge. This is a link that is loose or lost in many on-line programs. LeClair concludes that staff in the digital environment is enhanced by the on-site and adds that schools need to focus on: "How do we make sure we achieve the goals that the students had when they started the program?". What will change is the means for achieving such goals.

The new context has also provided a democratization of content through on-line platforms. FDC has made available an open, free platform that provides access to content produced by its professors, specialists and guests, with the aim of promoting reflections that contribute to social development. The new context reinforces FDC's strategy of placing the participant at the center of the learning and development process. Participants and organizations should increasingly look to business schools to support them in content curation and application, to access networks and to seek development for problem solving. The current context reinforces the signaling of "individualizing" the development process to the needs of the participant and lifelong learning.

Despite all the challenges imposed by current issues, FDC believes that there is only a way out if we consider collaboration, solidarity, ethics and trust. The most challenging moments invite us to revisit values. The answer lies in them. These have been guiding factors in FDC's strategies for the present and future, whether in practices, programs in progress or in the readjustment of the portfolio for the current moment. FDC believes (and implements in its programs) that, in order to promote sustainable growth, it is necessary to take care of all the stakeholders involved.

Part 4

MATTER OF LOOKING

Chapter 12

HOW BRAZIL IS PERCEIVED ABROAD

Human perception is frighteningly limited; we believe we are seeing the whole, when in fact we only see a fraction.

—Empedocles

Perception is not reality, but it says a lot about the image that is conveyed to outsiders. Many clichés about the country still circulate, such as Brazilians have "a reputation for being cordial but superficial," for being "afraid of the world," "an inferiority complex" and unprepared to face international competition. I believe that most people have stopped confusing us with Argentina, and no longer think that the capital of Brazil is Buenos Aires. Also, today's communication facilities have made us better known around the world. We are no longer recognized exclusively on the themes of soccer, carnival and samba.

Unfortunately, other negative factors have affected our image recently, especially regarding the issue of protecting the Amazon and uncontrolled deforestation. Not to mention some of President Bolsonaro's sayings and comments that have had very negative repercussions, and the security issue, which continues to be a negative point.

However, the space we occupy in the knowledge and imagination of people with a certain degree of imagination and curiosity is very far from making us known for the positive things we have accomplished. In the world press, however, mostly negative news has prevailed in the last few years.

I have always maintained that opinion about our country is formed from the inside out, and not the other way around. We have, admittedly, a devastating critical spirit, and those who visit us are surprised: when asked, we place great emphasis on our problems, and with some difficulty, and if asked with some insistence, we are able to remember positive aspects, some good things that show that in many areas we have progressed.

Sociologist Paulo Delgado, in an excerpt from his text "Brasil, Nobel do Pessimismo":

Brazil has to dedicate itself a little more to appreciating what it knows how to do. For the quality of everything that is discovered or invented today, especially technology, should be the subject of contracts on how it should be used, and not of patriotic speeches on whether or not it is appropriate. Everything that is service will be digital, all pollution will be monitored, and it is not possible to imagine a country without internal unity, political and business, to create its own legislation on the use of what commands the modern world.[1]

It is worth quoting the commentary in the book *Reflexões sobre a Política Externa Brasileira* (Reflections on Brazilian Foreign Policy), published in 1993 by the Instituto de Pesquisas em Relações Internacionais of the Fundação Alexandre de Gusmão.

In a world integrated by communications and with ever more extensive media networks, the dimension of the country's public image takes on fundamental importance. Not taking care of this issue in a prioritized, specific and professional manner has serious costs in terms of increasing difficulties for diplomatic action and governmental dialogue, resulting in a deterioration of the country's image. This question requires a twofold strategy; firstly, it would be necessary to make an effort to change the image of the country that has deteriorated greatly in the recent period. Such a change would have two moments: while economic stabilization and the resumption of growth are underway, encouragement would be given to a limited strategy aimed at avoiding further deterioration, and an offensive strategy would be prepared for when growth resumes. The second aspect would be to contemplate a permanent effort to publicize Brazil abroad, integrating all its possible dimensions. Such an effort would require not only its own administrative instance, but also the hiring of specialized services. It is recommended, therefore, the creation of a unit in Itamaraty that would concentrate information about Brazil and deal with the country's image and a specific program, in the MRE budget, with the necessary funding for contracting specialized services, in Brazil and abroad.[2]

---

1 Delgado, Paulo. *Brazil, Nobel Prize for Pessimism*. Available at: http://bit.ly/2OXyhmZ. Accessed on: 11 Dec. 2019.

2 P. 159.

The recent presidential election that brought back Lula to Brasilia certainly will be a fact.

Having participated in meetings abroad with some frequency, whether institutional or in contact with the business world, especially in the financial area, we noticed that the political situations were not commented on, other than exceptionally during the military regime of 1964 and that, even then, externally there was no unanimous criticism. To my surprise (and except for some specific radical groups), the receptivity was positive, recognizing that we had no alternative left at that time. Right now, the criticism for military intervention in the political system is almost unanimous.

Outside that period, the greatest difficulty I encountered in these contacts was the inflationary issue that, even in its most critical periods, caused a certain perplexity in our interlocutors. The constant question was about the possibility of investing and living with a country that did not have a reliable currency. Especially for long-term investors, this was a strong inhibiting factor for considering the country as an investment alternative. Fortunately, in recent years, we seem to be on our way to "civilized" inflation.

In the cultural field, especially in the musical area, popular and classical, Brazilian artists have always been exceptionally well received abroad, especially after the appearance of Bossa Nova, which established a new rhythm in the international musical space, projecting names like Tom Jobim, Chico Buarque, Vinícius de Moraes, Carlos Lyra, João Gilberto, Caetano Veloso, Maria Bethânia. With broad international projection we can also mention Heitor Villa-Lobos, Tarsila do Amaral, Cândido Portinari, Nélson Freire, Guiomar Novaes, Carlos Gomes, Francisco Mignone, Radamés Gnattali, João Carlos Martins, and, notably, the architect Oscar Niemeyer.

In Literature, Machado de Assis, Jorge Amado, Clarice Lispector, Carlos Drummond de Andrade, Monteiro Lobato, to name a few.

We had positive moments in the economic area during the so-called Brazilian miracle, with extraordinary growth rates, when it seemed that our country had really set the pace for sustainable growth and which, unfortunately, for a number of reasons, mostly of a political nature, have not been confirmed, although we have experienced some periods with a satisfactory growth rate.

The two terms of Fernando Henrique Cardoso and Luiz Inácio Lula da Silva, from the external point of view, were, for different reasons, of positive coexistence, despite the upsets that both had during their mandates, mainly due to external crises (the debt crisis in Latin American countries, in the case of FHC, and the consequences of the Lehman Brothers crisis of 2008, in the case of Lula).

But the general feeling that I have registered, in this period in which I have followed our image abroad more closely, is that we will continue to be seen as the country of the future, not being able to realize our enormous potential. Among the negative factors that are always remembered: the excessive political fragmentation, too many parties without a clearly defined ideological line, clear deficiencies in the area of education, fiscal management that has not shown consistency over different periods, leaving serious structural problems in the area of transportation and infrastructure in general, disorderly spending, critical problems in the area of sanitation and urban mobility. More recently, the fiscal situation of the country's accounts and a growing deficit have scared off international economists.

The uneven income distribution in Brazil, with a huge difference between the rich and poor, helps to create a negative image of our country abroad.

As mentioned before, despite all the problems we face, it is common sense that we have incredible growth potential, more than most public opinion realizes. With a highly critical view we focus mostly on our problems, which can be solved in due time.

In more recent years, the problems of corruption, which has always existed in different dimensions, have taken on unimaginable proportions, showing a rupture in the standards of ethical behavior involving political cadres, and, in general, the perverse behavior in different state-owned companies, which were truly looted.

Operation Car Wash (Operação Lava Jato), which had great international repercussion, had a huge impact on political life, affecting a large number of companies, committed to ethical misconduct by embezzling, clandestinely, resources to political parties, mainly to finance their political campaigns, the so-called Caixa 2 (Slush fund).

Thus, some of these companies that were at the forefront of this criminal process were forced to reduce their operations, some going into extrajudicial liquidation or even shutting down their activities.

When we thought that corruption, fiercely fought by Operation Car Wash, had been controlled, we had another huge frustration with the appearance of several cases of irregularities by state governments that, taking advantage of the absence of public bidding during the pandemic, made overpriced purchases of equipment produced abroad, which would be destined to save the lives of Brazilians.

As previously indicated, the framework for tourism is also an open question and internal security a negative factor in the country and does not contribute to attracting tourists, as well as representing an additional cost of protection for investors who consider investing resources in the country. International tourism is a long way from contributing to our growth and exploring what we have to offer.

It must be emphasized that, although it has not been possible to maintain a growth rate in the country that is compatible with our pressing needs, including job creation, the economic–financial management managed to keep inflation under control which, as we said before, had been in the past a major obstacle to attracting investments.

In fact, our low savings rate of around 15 percent, and that has been around 22 percent of GDP, is a chronic problem, and a fact that negatively influences our growth, not supplying the necessary resources. I also emphasize the relevance of foreign capital to our development in this specific area.

Recently, the exchange rate issue has been well managed, and the real has not lost substantial value—although recent losses can mainly be attributed to the external behavior of the dollar—and is no longer a source of major concern. Mario Henrique Simonsen, finance minister from 1974 to 1979, reminded us that "if inflation hurts, the exchange rate kills."

Coronavirus has had a strong impact on the exchange rate, due to the economic–financial and political implications of Covid-19 in the different countries affected. In our case, especially from March on, the consequence was a strong devaluation of our currency due to large sums of resources made available by government.

Thanks to the maintenance of large foreign exchange reserves and successive surpluses in the balance of trade, even despite all the internal difficulties, even so the flow of capital has been collaborating with the balance of payments, making a bearable deficit possible. An important factor was the positive trade balance due to agricultural and mining exports.

I would also mention another positive factor, the perception that the country needs to implement a set of reforms so that we can generate compatible economic growth, by leveraging the positive things we have internally. To this end, the great difficulty we face, which is not uncommon in countries with an early stage of democratic development, is the lack on part of politicians, of the need to accelerate these reforms, with the idea that the world is waiting such accomplishments.

Given what we are witnessing in this process of accelerated global changes, we must be aware that we are racing against time and that we need to focus on what is most relevant to be solved in the very short term. We cannot spend time on diverting attention to issues of little or no relevance and really focus on what is essential in our priorities, such as, for example, the different reforms on the government's agenda (administrative and fiscal reforms).

We must emphasize that Social Security Reform was certainly the greatest achievement of President Bolsonaro's first year in office, and that we were able to move forward with a project that had been dragging on for more than 30 years.

In summary, coming back to technology, I would say that there has been a large and substantial shift in the way Brazil is perceived abroad since the late 1950s, when I made my first forays abroad. Right now, it is clear that new technologies are fundamental.

It is worth remembering that the mobility for the circulation of capital that has come to characterize world markets in the last 30 years, with friendlier legislations to welcome foreign investments, was nonexistent.

From the turn of the century on, there was a noticeable change in the capital movements. The abundance of capital was noticeable and came to supply the so-called developing countries, which began to receive a greater volume of resources, including Latin American countries, whose finances were recovered after the great debt crisis that characterized the late 1990s, including with Brazil's moratorium.

The appearance of several international institutions that came to locate here, such as Morgan Stanley, JP Morgan, Merrill Lynch, Credit Suisse, following almost in real time what was happening here of importance, with the prominent presence of large international investment funds, in search of opportunities in our different markets, be it in debt securities or in equities, including private equity, with the big international players in this sector making their presence felt.

During the time I spent in New York as a *visiting scholar* in the second half of 2016 at Columbia University, when identifying myself as Brazilian, those more familiar with our successive political crises and their unfolding in the economic-financial area felt a disappointment. After all, a country with all our potential would not be able to find and take the initiatives that would allow it to grow again at sustainable rates, eliminating social inequalities.

Despite all the difficulties we face, we still managed, as mentioned before, to be a major recipient of foreign capital, notably, the largest in Latin America for some years.

Effectively, FDI had a positive flow of US$ 59 billion, in 2018, according to UNCTAD data. But the prevailing feeling is that this number could be multiplied a few times over, were this our internal picture. In 2019, FDI inflows into Brazil were still positive at US$75 billion, up 26 percent year-over-year, according to UNCTAD,[3] helping to mitigate the effects of other national accounts, allowing the current account deficit to remain in perfectly acceptable conditions, despite a drop in the trade balance. In 2022, due to

---

3 Available at: https://bit.ly/3pAxKDZ.

increased imports and decreased exports Brazil will have a smaller but still positive trade surplus, but FDI reached US$ 90.5 billion.

It is important to highlight the significant presence of Chinese investment in the country. In 2018, even though its appetite for investments in our region decreased 19 percent from the previous year, since 2005 Brazil has received 11 projects, with a total of US$28.9 billion, an amount lower than the one allocated to Venezuela (19 projects, US$ 67.2 billion).

I would say that the lack of knowledge about Brazil abroad has diminished, especially during Bolsonaro's term in office due to his nondemocratic behavior. It is difficult to have an external image different from the one we form. It is also difficult to imagine external perceptions different from those prevailing here, given the contacts with the Brazilian reality and with our opinion makers, apart from the actions of a press that plays, as it should, a critical role.

Markets move not only by facts that have happened or are measurable. Also of great relevance is the "trends" factor, i.e., what would be projected or under discussion. It is the projection of the future discounted to present value.

If it turns out that structural reforms are possible, there will gradually be a change in attitude toward investments in the country, which will obviously also depend on the international framework. Basically, if Brazilians do not believe on them, who will?

As we have mentioned, these decisions, whether on the side of entrepreneurs or individual investors, are strongly dependent on internal and external conjunctural aspects.

At the end of 2019 we were living an unprecedented picture with interest rates at their lowest level in decades, allowing a substantial reduction in the CDI (referential interest rate set by the Central Bank's Monetary Policy Committee), that caused this projected differential to fall substantially, stimulating the stock market and new launches.

As for the exchange rate, we must always look very carefully and not make predictions about its behavior and impact on investment decisions (this, of course, influences international trade and the repatriation of capital).

The substantial drop in the interest rate, which in 2016 was around 14 percent and in the month of August 2020 fell to 2 percent,[4] caused fixed income investments to lose their previous preeminence in Brazilian securities portfolios. On the other hand, domestic investors, who also have fixed income investments, migrated to the stock market and also to investing abroad to diversify their portfolio.

---

4 Kept until the Copom meeting on 10 December 2020.

Recently, after the pandemic and the war in Ukraine, the interest rate improved to a level not seen in the last 40 years.

Going to practical and obvious examples, the opening of the domestic market with tariff reductions, for the participation of foreign products and global markets, forced local companies to change their attitude toward their motivations of concentrating their activities exclusively in the domestic market. Even though this opening, which took place under Fernando Collor de Mello's government in the early 1990s, was less significant than some of our neighbors' in the region, it was still a warning sign for companies to change their policies, including considering partnerships here or abroad, as well as to take more aggressive positions in foreign markets. The exchange rate issue is another determining factor for these policies to momentarily have more or less weight in the business decision.

I have a positive view for the years ahead. President Lula is committed to fight poverty, which has reached alarming dimensions and will be on the top of the agenda of the new presidency. Inequality needs to be fiercely combated for our democratic system to prevail and to promote growth. That is what the majority of Lula's voters expect and are looking for.

Chapter 13

DOMESTIC AND INTERNATIONAL PRESS: ROLE OF THE DOMESTIC AND FOREIGN MEDIA COVERAGE OF BRAZIL'S INTERNATIONAL RELATIONS

Here in Brazil, in-house journalistic coverage on international themes focuses predominantly on specific issues, such as politics, economic behavior and extraordinary events that, for one reason or another, deserve space in the different vehicles because they are of interest to readers.

In the past, our major newspapers had numerous foreign correspondents. However, the loss of importance of the written media in the communication market made these journalists to return home with few exceptions.

The internet and social media also do not engage in broader coverage. They are also limited to current topics. On television, the situation is different, since Globo TV, which holds a substantial portion of the open and pay TV audience, has some important correspondents abroad, who provide coverage on themes different from those experienced, such as, for example, interviews with personalities from the academic and cultural world.

Now, with the entrance of CNN in the Brazilian market, bringing in its baggage a strong experience in world news, more space is opened for international coverage in our television media.

We must face reality. Very rarely have I come across the news abroad, in newspapers or on TV, with a positive view. However, some facts of this nature go unnoticed and do not gain space in the news.

Another factor is that many Brazilians who go abroad, in many cases, spread pessimistic views about the country. I am not advocating that we hide our ills, but a certain balance between the positive and the negative has to be sought.

The same goes for those who visit and interview us. We are always emphasizing our negatives and the challenges we face. When provoked, we are able to highlight our positive aspects.

My experience abroad is just the opposite. They always point out positive aspects of the country, and the problems only appear when asked.

A few years ago, in a meeting with Chileans from the public and private sector, after a great narrative of the positive aspects in the political–economic area, I couldn't resist the "epiphany" and asked: "Don't you have any problems?". As it turns out, they did, which have now erupted in the popular demonstrations and violent repression that have forced the government to promote radical changes and a constitutional referendum.

Perhaps a text by Ambassador Luiz Felipe Lampreia, from 1999, translates well what I feel about the subject:

> Today we have a free and vigorous press, which has played a very relevant role in this change of national life. I cannot help but observe, however, that, perhaps due to the magnitude of the internal challenges in Brazil, our media dedicate an excessively limited amount of space to issues of the country's international relations.
>
> In addition to realism, you have to work with a clear sense of history. What at one moment may seem like a bright avenue may soon turn into a dark cul-de-sac. Hence the need to invariably seek, in our external relations, the highest possible degree of autonomy. This has always been and continues to be a basic parameter of Brazilian diplomacy.
>
> Autonomy is not to be confused with isolation or self-sufficiency, but with the preservation of sufficient margins of choice and maneuverability so that we are able to follow the paths outlined by the will and the interests of the nation we serve.[1]

It is important to remember that in the case of Covid-19, the press was instrumental in getting the word out about the pandemic, and the examples of Lombardy, Milan, Bergamo, in Italy, as well as other European countries, and later New York, dominated the news.

Unfortunately, our image was shaken by the issue of environmental aggression and by the government, which made statements and adopted regressive and controversial policies, whose repercussions had a negative impact on the domestic press and abroad. By the way, the statistics released about forest fires were obviously very unfavorable and widely exploited by our local press.

---

1 Speech by Ambassador Luiz Felipe Lampreia to the graduating class of the Rio Branco Institute in 1999. He was also minister of Foreign Relations under Fernando Henrique Cardoso.

The pandemic worsened this picture by the presidency's insistence on a controversial policy to combat the virus and by the constant change of health ministers. The fact that Brazil is at the top of the list of countries affected by Covid-19 was definitely an indication that the country has not learned its lesson from what happened abroad.

Again, there is a great hope that the situation will have substantial changes in years ahead. Even before assuming power in January 2023, Lula was a prominent presence in COP27 and in his speeches he made clear that the question related to Amazonian deforestation and illegal activities will be on top of his government agenda. He also indicated the importance of international support for the purpose of overcoming such challenges.

Chapter 14

WHAT WAS IN THE MEDIA

The young man knows the rules, but the old man knows the exceptions.
—Oliver Wendell Holmes

They say that newspapers are running out of days. I am still an avid reader of daily printed news. I subscribe to four national newspapers that keep me company in the morning on a daily basis. Besides reading, I also have the habit of keeping newspaper clippings. The most present theme in my collection of published thoughts is related to the theme of international relations and the role of the Brazilian business community.

So, I selected some material that seemed relevant in the context of the book.

- A long interview granted by President Fernando Henrique Cardoso to Rádio Eldorado and transcribed by Estadão on 15 May 1997, entitled "Business diplomacy is irreplaceable (A diplomacia empresarial é insubstituível)";
- "Brazilian Multis will have 10 years to pay off debts (Multis brasileiras terão 10 anos para pagar dívidas)," in *O Estado de S. Paulo* (3 September 2013);[1]
- "Brazilian Multinationals (Multinacionais brasileiras)," from the Special Section of *Valor Econômico* (31 October 2012);
- "Brazilian companies now investing in the acquisition of foreign companies in the country (Empresas brasileiras agora investem na aquisição de estrangeiras no país)," in *O Estado de S. Paulo* (December 25, 2011);
- "Business Diplomacy Manifesto (Manifesto da diplomacia empresarial)," written by Marcos Troyjo for *Valor Econômico*;

---

1 Available at: http://bit.ly/37uF51K.

- "Brazilian isolationism (O isolacionismo brasileiro)," *in O Estado de S. Paulo*, written by Gustavo Franco, on 26 August 2018;
- "Is the Bolsonaro government's foreign policy on the right track? (A política externa do governo Bolsonaro está no caminho certo?)" *Folha de S.Paulo* (18 January 2020).

What do these articles have in common and how are they related to the themes of this book? Starting with Fernando Henrique Cardoso's long interview, the former president emphasizes the relevance in presidential functions of international diplomacy. Our former head of state had this sensitivity, and I witnessed his personal involvement in issues that jeopardized our association with Mercosur, at critical moments of our commercial coexistence with our partners, especially Argentina.

Finally, Fernando Henrique Cardoso reminded us that the relationship between countries should not be limited to exclusively commercial issues. We see today that, with free exchange rates and open markets, the flow of investments has increased brutally, not only by the so-called direct investments (FDI) that Brazil has intensively pursued, but also portfolio investments, which occupy a relevant space in the stock exchanges and financial markets, influencing their long-term trends and short-term volatility.

The topic of globalization, raised by journalist Ruy Mesquita on the occasion, is still on the agenda. Some claim that we are entering a phase of de-globalization. Others prefer to call it re-globalization. In reality, the election of Trump with his revisionism, criticism of trade agreements and the WTO, tariff wars and the return of protectionism, sometimes camouflaged, not to mention the emergence of China as a major player on the world stage, have created a set of new factors whose consequences we will still take some time to measure. Hopefully, the Trump era is over, but opinions on trade issues may have permanently shifted.

We have, on one hand, the tax issue as a relevant factor in the decision of Brazilian companies to invest abroad, as well as this behavior is very much linked not only to issues related to the domestic market, for example, a drop in demand and exchange rate behavior that stimulates imports, as well as opportunistic acquisitions that may happen when good opportunities arise.

The article by Marcos Troyjo, who, when we started this text, was the special secretary for Foreign Trade and International Affairs at the Economy Ministry and was unanimously elected president of the BRICS Bank is still very current. Looking back over the past 15 years, it is hard to disagree that many of the aspects he indicated are not still present. Among some, we cite: the Fourth Industrial Revolution, anarchic financial flows, protectionist armor (Trumpism), the difficulty of continuing to finance development by putting government roles in place, the need for greater participation in international trade, low representation of the country in the international press (we only appear with the crises), unsatisfactory role of the Brazilian needs, difficulty to communicate in English, among others. It is necessary to read the entire article to see that we are still dealing with the same problems and that we will continue to need a long-term policy as we have tried to point out throughout this study.

Also, from political analyst and Professor Marcos Troyjo, it is worth quoting part of his article published in September 2018 in *Brazilian Problems (Problemas Brasileiros):*

> In Brazil, we confuse foreign policy, diplomacy, and international insertion. They are not the same thing. Diplomacy is an activity between states, restricted to chancelleries. For foreign policy, other elements need to be added, such as defense policy. And international insertion means the fine tuning between private sector actors, government, and diplomacy to increase the wealth of a given country.[2]

The economist Gustavo Franco, who was president of the Central Bank from 1997 to 1999, translated all this into Brazilian isolationism. He statistically points out that in 1960 our current account of trade in exports and imports was 18 percent as a percentage of GDP. In China, respectively, 9.5 and 8.7 percent. Over the next 20 years what do we have: the most open Korea grew to 38.3 percent in 1970 and to 67.2 percent in 1980. Brazil did not advance and stood at 19.2 percent in 1980. In 2010, Korea reached 82.5 percent while Planet Earth reached 47.7 percent. Our degree of openness in 2017 was 18.3 percent, virtually the same as in 1960.

Many international relations analysts, at the time of the discussions started by specialized press agencies, indicated that the next president would have a fragile international scenario in which to seek a greater role for Brazil and little time for a positive and realistic agenda for the country, due to an adverse international framework, aggravated by the conflict between the United States and China, and where the Asian superpower is concerned, more modest growth for the coming years, with internal and external consequences yet to be measured. Unfortunately, these projections eventually came true, made worse by the devastating coronavirus that emerged in China.

Thus, the issue of Brazilian foreign policy has never been so debated and questioned due to the polemics that have arisen since Minister Ernesto Araújo

---

2 Available at: http://bit.ly/3uddHzl. Accessed on: 4 Aug. 2019.

took office at Itamaraty. In early 2020, the 18 January *Folha de S.Paulo* put the Bolsonarist foreign policy into debate, asking the question: "Is Bolsonaro's foreign policy on the right track?". The question was sent to Ambassador Rubens Ricupero and international relations analyst Alberto Pfeifer, for each one to present a different point of view about the Itamaraty's performance in the period.[3]

For Ricupero,

Bolsonarist diplomacy has a rotten finger, it systematically errs in assessing situations. This is why the president gets it right more when he goes backwards than when he goes forwards. The list of absurdities abandoned or corrected is enormous: offering bases to the USA, announcement of withdrawal from the Paris climate agreement; intention to move the embassy from Tel Aviv to Jerusalem; hostile statements to the Chinese and the Arabs; Eduardo Bolsonaro's frustrated nomination as ambassador to Washington; and betting on failed alliances (Macri, Salvini, Netanyahu, Chilean Piñera, Venezuelan Juan Guaidó).

The ambassador goes further and complements the harsh critical view on the international performance of the Bolsonaro government:

The political personality cultivated by the president, his children, and advisors is characterized by internal and external aggressiveness. It is the opposite of the "diplomatic" qualities required by international coexistence. Unfortunately, the chancellor aggravates rather than compensates for this "antidiplomacy."

Pfeifer, on the other hand, presents a favorable view, praising "the pragmatism and coherence" committed by the government.

Bolsonaro proposed the liberal conduct of the economy, enhancing the operation of market logic and free enterprise, and reducing the role of the state. Its social-political agenda is of a conservative matrix, the primacy of Western Christian values, the fight against communism, and the confrontation of crime and corruption. Its stance in multilateral forums has followed this orientation in the field of moral behavior.

---

3 Available at: https://bit.ly/2MagYOq.

And he ends by saying:

> Given the proper discounting of the novitiate of management, the con-
> clusion is that the routing is satisfactory. There were advances on the
> economic and political agenda. In international relations, the only fatal
> mistake is irreversibility, which leads to the cessation of dialogue and con-
> flict. Mistaken acts have proven to be repairable, such as the hasty stance
> on the Venezuelan issue and the relocation of the embassy to Israel.

In a speech at Firjan on 28 August 2019, Minister Ernesto Araújo made clear
his vision of foreign policy and the role of businessmen.

> I think I continue to learn this every day, as do the other team
> members—because this is also another element that we are learning:
> I think that, for the first time, we have a government in Brazil that
> works as a team, that is a team, and not a system of assigning functions
> according to certain political arrangements; without prejudice to all the
> quality of policies that there were in the past, despite a system that had
> these characteristics, and without prejudice to all the people who have
> always worked on these previous schemes, among which I modestly
> include myself, of course (I worked for 30 years in the public service),
> but today we realize that this was one of Brazil's problems, one of the
> problems we tried to overcome.
>
> In this previous framework, of a distribution of the State according
> to power schemes, Itamaraty and foreign policy were a kind of "foreign
> body," an organ that was there and did not get in the way, that "organized
> trips" and that, from time to time, had a greater or lesser participation
> in commercial policy, in other schemes, but was very much seen by
> Brazilian society itself as a foreign body. This is another commitment
> I have had since my appointment: to make Itamaraty a part of the
> national project, a part of the government, and not a "spaceship that by
> chance landed in Brasilia."
>
> Going back a bit to the subject of the sources of knowledge: today it is
> paradoxical, because we have access, thanks to technology, to practically
> inexhaustible sources and immediate information and knowledge, and
> yet we don't use them, or we use them poorly, also because we are
> becoming aware (another task that we must learn every day) of how
> much manipulation there is in this circulation of information.

By transcribing part of the speech, we try to discuss positions that are exclusive to these personalities, but that are echoed by many other "experts" and

different entities, most of which are always critical of the "new" foreign policy!

In an interview I conducted with the chancellor at the Itamaraty Palace in February 2020, he commented:

> [...] the political system, which is precisely one of the great things we are trying to break in this government. I think that the political-patrimonialist system, which has been running us for so long, produces a country afraid of the world; a country shy.
>
> [...] (our politicians are totally isolated from the world) because it is a system that is very comfortable for the political elite, who end up somehow controlling the economic fruits. The traditional system here is still in place, but we are trying to break it. So I think that this ability of the system, over the centuries, to create a possibility for the elites to control the economy, even having a state economy, fully through all kinds of manipulation, legislation, regulation, produces a shrunken country. It is all part of this mentality, this political system. We really had a great economy, but run by a very corporate political apparatus, and very primitive in a way, where we never really had a politics of ideas; it had to be a politics of positions. The politicians are there to get some position that will enable them to have a job, that will carry resources, sustain themselves in exchange for one favor for another. State owned, more state owned, less state owned, but always a somewhat state owned economy.

With the replacement at the head of the Foreign Ministry of Ernesto Araújo by Carlos França, another career diplomat, there was a substantial change in policies and behavior, favoring a more traditional and measured approach to foreign relations, but not marking his mandate with any extraordinary measures due to the circumstances. He has attended several international meetings during his term and made Brazil visible again.

One of the first members of President Lula's cabinet to be announced is our next foreign minister, Ambassador Mauro Vieira; Vieira is an accomplished diplomat, a former ambassador to Buenos Aires, to Washington and to the United Nations, as well as minister for foreign affairs under President Dilma Rousseff. Celso Amorim, president Lula's former foreign minister, is likely to be influential in the new administration as well.

Part 5

THE MULTIPLE FACES OF INTERNATIONALIZATION

Chapter 15

BRAZIL ON THE MIGRATION MAP

Migration out of necessity is at the root of mankind's nomadism. Historical studies tell us that, in pre-civilization eras, human groupings were not sedentary because they always had to search for food in new locations. However, millennia later, part of humanity still must migrate out of necessity. And, surprisingly, the search for food remains one of the reasons for large groups to move.

But that is not all. Add to food insecurity the well-founded fear of persecution for reasons of race, religion, nationality, social group or political opinions, or even serious and widespread human rights violations.

These motivations have been so present since the last century that they ended up receiving a specific nomenclature to designate such international movements of people who are forcibly displaced from their place of residence. The term is "refugee."

There are also voluntary migrations. Among the reasons, one can cite the search for better pay and quality of life, personal affinity or tourism. Regardless of the reason that leads human beings to migrate, the fact is that, in 2019, the largest source of foreign capital to developing countries was not FDI, but rather remittances from migrants to their countries of origin, according to data from the World Bank, reaching values close to US$700 billion.[1]

Surprisingly to many analysts in 12 months (till August 2022) the level of remittance for Mexicans grew 20 percent and set a new record of US$ 56.2 billion.

July 2022 remittances reached a record of US$ 5.3 billion. The projection for the year is US$ 60 billion.

---

1 Flow of Money from Migrants Already Exceeds Foreign Investment. *Valor Econômico*, São Paulo, 10 Sept. 2019.

That represents an important source of support for foreign accounts of Mexico, representing around 4.1 percent of their GDP. In other Central American countries, we have a similar situation.

According to the Inter-American Dialogue (IAD), a Washington, DC-based think tank, family remittances to Latin American and Caribbean countries grew by 10 percent in 2018, one of the highest rates recorded since the financial crisis of the previous decade. According to the group, the high rates of international remittances contrast with the poor economic growth rates, which in the same year, for example, averaged a 1.9 percent increase for the countries in the region. In Haiti, the ratio of international remittances to GDP reached 37 percent in 2020.[2]

However, while tourism tends to be well liked, the settlement of foreigners in other countries is not always well received.

Numbers

According to the United Nations High Commissioner for Refugees (UNHCR), by the end of 2019, 79.5 million people have been forced to relocate (1 percent of the world's population). Of this total, 26 million are classified as refugees. Of the total, 68 percent of them come from five countries: Syria, Venezuela, Afghanistan, South Sudan and Myanmar. Overall, 73 percent choose to move to neighboring countries. In these cases, these are Turkey, Colombia, Brazil, Pakistan and Uganda.[3]

In 1951, the UN Convention relating to the Status of Refugees defined the term in Article 1, referring to a person who:

> fearing persecution for reasons of race, religion, nationality, social group or political opinion, is outside the country of his nationality and is unable to or, owing to such fear, does not wish to avail himself of the protection of that country, or that, if he has no nationality and is outside the country in which he had his habitual residence as a result of such events, he is unable or, owing to such fear, does not wish to return to it.[4]

In 1967, the organization created a diplomatic protocol concerning refugees, focusing on those who escaped the scourge of World War II. As a result,

---

2 Available at: https://www.bbc.com/portuguese/internacional-56342515.
3 *UNHCR*. Available at: http://bit.ly/37vZPWJ.
4 *UN. Convention relating to the Status of Refugees. 1951. Article 1° (2)*. Available at: https://bit .ly/3aArzLZ. Accessed on: 10 Sept. 2019.

refugees received greater protection and could not be deported back to their country of origin.

Also according to UNHCR data, there are a total of 45.7 million who are internally displaced (live in temporary shelters, fleeing conflicts, environmental disasters, etc.). Outside of this count, there are an estimated 4.2 million stateless persons, i.e., people who are not recognized by any national state.

In the context of a globalized world, issues related to transnational displacement have been occupying more space in the foreign policy of many countries, especially those most sought after by refugees.

Brazil in the World

In Brazil, this process of repositioning countries, and their population, in the global political economy arouses more and more interest in the discussions of international migration. Issues concerning our international relations in general, institutional or individual, have never been widely discussed, either on the agenda of our elites or of our congressmen. It is also a fact that we send more people abroad than we receive, a subject that has always caught the attention of our press. Despite all these factors, and even though we are far from the world's conflict regions, we are still the sixth most common country in the world for refugee requests.

2018 was the year in which Brazil received the most refugee requests: 80,000, 75 percent of them Venezuelans. In smaller numbers, also Angolans, Nepalese, Haitians and Syrians. There is a shortage of public policies, financial reserves and qualified personnel. An important role in mitigating refugee problems is played by civil society, churches, schools and universities.

In 2022, there was a growing number of Afghans coming to Brazil, particularly to São Paulo, escaping from the Taliban. Most of them arrived and stayed unassisted at Guarulhos International Airport, helped by social institutions and private individuals who are doing their best to minimize their discomfort while local government defines a policy to cater to their needs.

Since we are geographically distant from the main conflict regions of the world in Africa and Asia, the refugee issue does not touch us directly. Because of this, those who arrive here have a different profile: good educational background, with more than 30 percent having a college degree! They bring knowledge and know-how that can be useful for the country, but their absorption by our community is hindered by the unemployment we are facing.

Our country was historically formed by immigrants: Portuguese conquerors and workers, enslaved Africans and later European immigrants, who arrived here during the period of the great migrations (1880–1930).

To a lesser extent, we also receive from other regions of origin, such as South and Southeast Asia and the Middle East. It is also worth remembering the migrants who fled World War II, political activists from Europe and Latin America, who escaped from political crises in their respective countries (Argentina, Venezuela, Chile, Peru, Bolivia and most recently Cuba).

Similarly, Brazil was the focus of emigration during the period of military dictatorship (1964–85), when several political activists were forced to leave the country and go into exile abroad.

From the 1980s on, Brazil repositioned itself in the world political economy as an exporter of migrants, while also attracting migrants from Latin America, Asia and Africa, either for political reasons or in search of better job opportunities.

Recent studies bring the discussion between transnational migration and the ongoing concern of nation-states in selecting desirable and undesirable immigrants. In this sense, the flow of migration in some countries creates an issue concerning adaptation and reception. In some specific situations, the theme was (and is being) treated as a "social problem," even with a certain amount of hysteria by national residents, with xenophobic manifestations of the most varied kinds.

The United States continues to be a country that exerts a strong attraction for Brazilians who seek a future in the land of Uncle Sam. In 2018, 4,400 Brazilians migrated to the United States legally, to work or study, representing a 27.3 percent increase over the previous year.[5] However, the rigidity of the migration policy implemented by President Donald Trump has made life for Brazilians who choose to enter that country illegally very difficult. The number of repatriates in 2019 was a record: almost 18,000! By February 2020, more than 370 Brazilians had already been forced to return to Brazil.[6] The number was surpassed in the first nine months of 2022.

Given the magnitude of the processes of international migration and the intensification of the circulation of foreigners coming for the most varied reasons, the states, especially those most sought after by migrants, increase the degree of surveillance and border control, creating categories of "legal" and "regular" migrants on the one hand, and "illegal," "irregular" or "undocumented" migrants.

The change in international conditions, accelerated by globalization, stimulates populism around the world, bringing in its wake antiforeigner

---

5 Brazilians seek the American dream through the front door. *O Globo*, Rio de Janeiro, 8 Sept. 2019.

6 See more at: http://bit.ly/2NK6OnP.

sentiment, turning them into villains for "stealing jobs" and "disfiguring" national entities. Obviously, the position makes no sense, as people in the search for a new life has never exceeded 3 percent in the last 50 years.

Brazilians Leaving Brazil

The data on Brazilians abroad is not complete due to illegal migration flows. Some data, however, help to understand the current scenario a little. According to a 2018 survey by the Department of Economic and Social Affairs of the United Nations Secretariat, about 1.5 million Brazilians were living outside the country in the first half of 2017, with the majority residing in European countries.

On the Old Continent, Brazilians migrated mainly to Portugal and Spain. Those who tried to enter illegally, by air or land, faced a high rate of rejection at the strict checkpoints and, in some cases, abuse from the authorities of the countries they wanted to enter. Canada and Australia have also been countries in demand and have accepted our emigrants in the past.

In more recent years, emigration to Portugal has attracted growing flows from our middle class, due to the domestic conjuncture of high unemployment, with, in several cases, families also choosing to leave the country due to precarious security conditions in some Brazilian capitals. In 2018, many Brazilians were barred at the border, with the largest number being in the 35–39 age group. There are 105,423 Brazilians with residence permits in Portugal, 62,575 of whom are women.

Entry of Foreigners to Brazil—The Immigrant's Importance for Brazilian Culture and Progress

As previously mentioned, Brazil is a country of immigrations. Our population results from an interconnection and mixture of multiple origins of blood and nationality. Without getting into the discussion on the theme of "racial democracy," which is a topic that can be argued at length and with passion, it is interesting to take a brief look at the main groups that came here to seek a home in previous decades, even with a certain degree of encouragement from our governments at the time.

• Italian immigration

By 1920, the state of São Paulo had received approximately 70 percent of the Italian immigrants who came to Brazil. Most of them were bound for the coffee farms because the state subsidized the cost of the tickets. In 2013, there were approximately 1.5 million Italians and their descendants living in São Paulo, representing 34 percent of the state's population. The first immigrants date back to 1870. The end of slavery was a determining factor for the arrival of immigrants.

- **Japanese immigration**

Japanese immigration to Brazil "officially" began at the beginning of the twentieth century, in 1908. Brazil has reached the largest population of Japanese origin outside Japan, with about 1.5 million so-called Nikkei. Today they are totally adapted to Brazilian life, just like the Italians, Spanish, Germans and Portuguese.

- **Spanish immigration**

In the nineteenth and twentieth centuries there was a large Spanish migratory flow to Brazil, representing the third largest contingent that chose the country as a second homeland.

- **Portuguese immigration**

Portuguese immigration arrived in Brazil with the discovery in 1500, with the first settlers. However, migration to Brazil became significant in the eighteenth century, with the development of mining in the colonial economy, when hundreds of thousands of settlers arrived here. After independence, in the first half of the nineteenth century, immigration stagnated. It grew again in the second half of the century, reaching its peak in the first half of the twentieth century, when 25,000 Portuguese arrived here annually.

- **Other flows**

It is worth mentioning the German migration that occurred in the nineteenth and twentieth centuries to various regions of the country, especially in the south. It is estimated that between 1824 and 1972, about 260,000 Germans entered Brazil, the fifth largest nationality that migrated to our country.

Jewish immigration began with the colonization of Brazil, when Sephardic Jews and New Christians settled in the colonies.

It is important to highlight the Arab immigration, which occurred mainly at the end of the nineteenth century. Most of the immigrants were of Lebanese origin. Interestingly, today there are more Lebanese in São Paulo than in the capital of Lebanon, Beirut!

In some moments of a more recent past, there was a greater additional Portuguese migration in the aftermath of their political Revolution in 25 April 1974 and, episodically, a greater flow of Argentines, Chileans, Paraguayans, Peruvians and especially Bolivians, during economic (or even political) crises in their respective countries and who sought, in our country, opportunities for better days. As far as I remember, the so-called regional migrations did not cause any noises or grumblings within the country about a supposed "invasion of foreigners" and were generally well received.

What I noted, additionally, was that, in many cases, and up to this day, this applied mostly to Bolivians, exploited in informal jobs and, in some situations, in subhuman conditions, with miserable salaries and unacceptable working conditions.

We also had the most relevant migration of Haitians and, mainly, Syrians, due to the great civilization crises in their respective countries in the last five years.

Some industrial groups have mobilized to help the immigrants, in addition to the involvement of the different churches.

In the case of the Syrians, given the existence of a local community of compatriots, their adaptation, whether by learning our language or by looking for jobs, was facilitated. The Haitians, according to available information, have also been absorbed, either in service activities in the city or in the countryside.

The gateway, when there was a greater flow, was through our northern border. Obviously, the language issue has also been a factor that hinders this migration and search for work.

The Drama of Venezuelans

The terrible and inhumane humanitarian conditions that have been observed in Venezuela, especially after the death of Chávez, and his succession by Maduro, have given the migration issue a dimension that we had not seen before. In the case of Venezuela, more than 3.6 million have been displaced since 2015, most living in Latin American and Caribbean countries. It is the largest influx in Latin American history. Few are recognized as refugees, but rather as economic migrants. However, the collapse of the country is no ordinary crisis, resembling a humanitarian catastrophe. Maintaining the current migration flow from Venezuela, it is estimated that by 2020/2021 the number would be greater than the migrants who left Syria after the start of the war.

Brazil has opened its doors to the contingent of neighboring migrants, which is concentrated, for obvious reasons, in the north of the country, particularly in the border state of Roraima, especially in the city of Pacaraima.

According to data made available by ACNUR to our research, in September 2020, 4,518 refugees and migrants were living in shelters in Roraima, and 1,350 participated in the voluntary internalization program. As of 30 August 2020, the number counted was 102,504 Venezuelan refugee applicants and 148,782 Venezuelan men and women with temporary or definitive residence visas in Brazil. They are people with no prospect of returning to their country in the short or medium term.[7,8,9]

I was in Pacaraima in May 2019. I witnessed that the increasing number of Venezuelans arriving at the border had created a social and humanitarian problem in that city. The state was not prepared or structured to give an adequate welcome to these migrants. The region is geographically isolated from the rest of Brazil and, as a result, has few economic opportunities. The ever-increasing population flow highlights the great vulnerability of the people who are arriving, affecting the absorption capacity of the border communities, especially of public services.

They left everything behind, in search of survival, coming from a country devastated by hunger, without the minimal conditions for a dignified life, as a result of crises in hospitals, lack of medicine and the total loss of the value of its currency, with inflation that recently reached figures above 1 million percent annually, with unemployment and a reduction in the GDP, which today is one-third of what it was before.

In this context, the government of President Temer released extraordinary resources, as well as mobilizing different ministries to collaborate in the process of absorbing this flow of Venezuelan brothers and sisters and engage the UN system seeking to strengthen its actions. The same continued during Bolsonaro's government.

The UNHCR, a United Nations agency with outstanding performance in different countries, has been playing a very relevant role in the countries where the migratory flows have been more critical, and with an outstanding performance in the north of the country, in total harmony with the military located in the region. UNHCR supports the three pillars of the federal policy: documentation, emergency assistance and integration actions. Venezuelans have two options: refuge or temporary residence permit. It is fundamental for the integration program to seek volunteers for internalization, transferring those already regularized in Roraima to other Brazilian states, where there are better and greater possibilities for integration. I am part of a

---

7 Available at: https://bit.ly/2Nl5E2t.
8 Available at: https://bit.ly/3awo3lI.
9 Available at: http://bit.ly/3ufdBXK.

multidisciplinary segment called the Mobilizing Committee, which aims to facilitate the reception of Venezuelans in our country.

It is worth remembering that Brazil has always played a pioneering and leading role in the international protection of refugees. It was the first country in the Southern Cone to ratify the 1951 Convention relating to the Status of Refugees, in 1960, and was also one of the first countries to join the UNHCR Executive Committee, responsible for approving the agency's annual programs and budgets.

It works in total harmony with other philanthropic entities, such as: Caritas Internationalis, International Red Cross, Doctors Without Borders and AVSI (an Italian non-governmental organization (NGO) with a significant contingent in Pacaraima). As I also mentioned before, different religions are also represented. Worthy of mention too are the different agencies of the Ministry of Justice, Citizenship, Health and the Federal Police. Special mention should be made of the Armed Forces which, besides the logistical aspects, play a very important role in maintaining order in Boa Vista and Pacaraima.

Until a few years ago, this issue did not sensitize our society. Now it is justifiably the object of double concern. Firstly, because of the negative reaction of some groups that are not at all receptive to welcoming refugees, allegedly due to the high level of unemployment we face. On the other hand, the country has to structure itself for a new reality to which we cannot omit ourselves, and our recognized humanitarian values must prevail.

It bears repeating: the UN considers it one of the largest forced displacement crises on the planet, with about four million displaced people as of June 2019. In Brazil, 80,000 refugee requests have been filed.

The world is not experiencing a refugee crisis, but a crisis for refugee people. It is more humane to open borders than to close them!

The pandemic will certainly bring very perverse consequences for those who seek to relocate to the various regions. If many countries had already implemented increasingly restrictive policies, this situation could be even more rigid, with borders being closed indefinitely.

The NGO World Vision is "deeply concerned" that the impacts of Covid-19 could "permanently scar the development of a generation of the world's most vulnerable children," according to World Vision International president and CEO Andrew Morley. He refers mainly to children who will be most affected due to the high infant mortality rate.[10] It had been falling but may rise again. In lower-income countries, children are left unprotected due to

---

10 Available at: https://blog.visaomundial.org/resposta-COVID19-fase2/.

poor sanitation conditions, showing great vulnerability. They are then faced with a difficult choice: risk exposure to the virus or starve to death. World Vision International seeks resources from wealthier countries to mitigate the perverse effects of Covid-19 and preserve the lives of these unprotected children.

The migration issue will be strongly affected by the pandemic with closed borders and unemployment, creating even greater difficulties for those who want to move. Another consequence is that countries where families rely heavily on remittances sent by expatriates will suffer, as many of them may lose their jobs. The Central American countries, for example, will be greatly affected!

This scenario was deeply aggravated by the war in Ukraine. A large percentage of its population, as much as 40 percent according to estimates, emigrated mainly to Poland and other neighboring countries. A great number of the refugees were children. The question is whether and when they will return to their countries. The reconstruction of the country, once the war is over, will demand large sums of money. An initiative like the Marshall Plan, created after World War II, is under discussion for Ukraine recovery.

Chapter 16

IN SOCCER, WE ARE MORE DARING

It may be strange to discuss soccer in the context of the internationalization of Brazil, which was purposely included in the wake of the migration issue. We must recognize that soccer made our country became better known abroad. For a long time, we were known as the country of soccer, along with samba schools and *mulatto* women, and a certain sexual freedom, which unfortunately created a distorted image of our country.

In issue 99 (2013), of *Revista da USP*,[1] we have a scholarly publication entirely dedicated to soccer. I selected an article that summarizes well the importance of soccer for Brazilian society.

> Initially an elite sport, soccer was soon "taken over" by the lower classes. Embedded in a black-mestizo-based cultural broth that operated at the margins of "official" society—the spheres of politics, citizenship, and the market—soccer has been reinvented based on a different kind of bodily intelligence. At the same time, it activated the forces of oral tradition and emerging mass culture, becoming a powerful mythical narrative of the country.[2]

I believe that lately this image has become outdated, even though carnival and soccer continue to be identified with our country.

When it comes to Brazilian soccer, being international is synonymous with high status. Among clubs, for many years, Santos and São Paulo boasted of their unique world champion status. Then Corinthians joined the select group.

Besides the pecking order among national rivals, I am reminded that all of us who travel abroad certainly face that classic soccer question when we

---

1 Available at: https://www.revistas.usp.br/revusp/issue/view/5861.
2 Kaz, Leonel et al. Handling the Ball: Soccer and Brazil. *Revista USP*, No. 99, pp. 67–78, 2013.

identify ourselves as Brazilians. Invariably, Pelé's name appears prominently. But it isn't the only name often remembered. Other stars are mentioned, such as: Zagallo, Romário, Bebeto, Taffarel, Rivelino, Sócrates, Neymar, Falcão, Zico, Careca.

However, for me, it was with some surprise when I was at an IBM seminar in Russia, in St. Petersburg, and decided to go back from the convention center to the hotel where I was staying riding a rickshaw, pedaled by a young Russian. When I identified myself as Brazilian, he, after mentioning our soccer as world champions, made reference to the star player who had impacted him most strongly: Rogério Ceni, São Paulo's goalkeeper. I cannot, in any way, fail to recognize in that athlete his exceptional qualities (including taking free kicks and penalty kicks), but his quote was amazing! Ceni is now the coach of São Paulo Futebol Clube.

Going straight to the subject that justifies the inclusion of the soccer theme and its internationalization, soccer players are a valuable export "commodity" for the country. After all, the world of soccer moves a significant amount of resources around the globe. In the specific case of Brazil, the most relevant movements I believe have been the transfer of players like Neymar (signed initially by Barcelona and later traded to Paris Saint-Germain). Our biggest business partners are European clubs. Among the countries that are the most prominent in signing our athletes are Spain, Italy and Germany.

More recently, other countries have started importing our "Made in Brazil" players, including Arab states as well as China, where soccer is becoming increasingly popular. The big clubs in the Asian giant are willing to pay huge sums of money to sign foreign players. Some stay for long periods, while others, after a trial run, sometimes do not adapt or are relegated and traded back.

In a ranking released by FIFA regarding the market for players in the year 2020, Brazil led the list in two aspects: quantity and value. There were 2,008 transactions, which totaled US$ 734 million.[3]

We have a new reality of older players who are coming home, while clubs here and abroad invest in younger players, those who sign because they anticipate a great future. Even some acquisitions are made in the so-called base groups, when they are not yet stars, but are seen as having great potential. In many cases, they sign a contract, but they stay around until they reach a certain age and then they can leave for the clubs that have invested in them.

---

3 Available at: http://bit.ly/3bzGbKK.

Some of these athletes will return to Brazil, though only the "rich" teams have had the financial conditions to bring them back, late in their careers if at all. Thus, the group of "buyers" is limited and led by Flamengo, Palmeiras, São Paulo, Corinthians and Internacional from Rio Grande do Sul. These are clubs that have a large number of admirers, earning good income from their matches. Television rights are an important source of income for the clubs.

If Brazil exports players, it also imports from different countries, mainly from South America, which has supplied a good number of athletes. This is partly due to the advantages of the exchange market, which gives our currency a comparatively higher value than that of neighboring countries. Among the main ones are Argentina, Uruguay, Chile, Colombia, Ecuador and even Venezuela. Some foreign coaches have also been occupying space in Brazilian soccer, particularly Portuguese, as is the case of Jorge Jesus, who was at Flamengo, the most recognized. Some players come on a loan basis for a certain period of time, with an option to renew or even sell.

The post-Covid-19 international landscape will affect soccer. The issue of player transfers will most likely, in the short term, decrease substantially. And, as a consequence, the value of the transfer fees. Some reports show how muddled the midfield in soccer has become. On 8 May 2020, the newspaper *O Estado de S. Paulo* published a report focusing on the decline of the market value of clubs and players during the pandemic. This report warned about the beating suffered by the ball market in the pandemic situation, based on a study by KPMG consulting. The estimate was a drop of more than 20 percent in contracts, including for players like Neymar and Lionel Messi.[4] The following month, on 12 June, the newspaper went back to the issue and brought an interview with the lawyer with more than two decades of experience in the soccer market, Marcos Motta. For him, the market will lose R$ 11 billion, mainly with player transfers.[5]

The figures for these transactions are not fully available, and in some cases commented on by the press, the authenticity and transparency of these figures has been questioned. There are even tax hang-ups that our tax authorities have investigated.

As indicative values, the most expensive transfers of Brazilian players were as follows:

---

4 Available at: https://www.goal.com/en/news/100-most-expensive-football-transfers -all-time/ikr3oojohla51fh9adq3qkwpu.

5 Market Will Lose R $ 11 billion from Purchases. *O Estado de S. Paulo*, 12 June 2020, p. A 12.

MOST EXPENSIVE TRANSFERS OF BRAZILIAN PLAYERS IN FOOTBALL HISTORY (TOP 5)

	Player	Position	From	To	Value (million €)	Year
1	Neymar	Forward	Barcelona (ES)	Paris Saint-Germain (FR)	222	2017
2	Philippe Coutinho	Midfielder	Liverpool (UK)	Barcelona (ES)	145	2017
3	Neymar	Forward	Santos (BR)	Barcelona (ES)	88.2	2013
4	Arthur	Midfielder	Barcelona (ES)	Juventus (IT)	72	2020
5	Diego Costa	Forward	Chelsea (UK)	Chelsea–Atletico Madrid (ES)	66	2018

Source: Transfermarkt, 2022.[6]

In the 2022 list of the 10 most expensive transfers in soccer (top 10), Neymar appears twice, followed by another Brazilian, Coutinho (a member of our national team) from Liverpool to Barcelona.

In mid-December Palmeiras announced that 16-year-old player Endrick signed a contract with Club Real Madrid for a sum of R\$ 407 million or about US\$ 85 million. He will play in Brazil until he reaches the age of 18.

The figures cited below serve to indicate the relevance of soccer in the so-called ball market, which represents incredible sums of money, not to mention the promotion of Brazilian players in the world context.

The Board of Registrations and Transfers of the Brazilian Football Confederation (CBF) has consolidated the figures for the first seven months of 2019. We have the following table: 12,493 domestic transfers were registered. Abroad, there were 1,484. From external transfers, encompassing professional, indoor soccer and amateur players, $210,962,623 euros were collected. On the import side, the national clubs invested almost R\$ 270 million in hiring players from other countries. There were 983 athletes from outside Brazil. The only countries that did not have foreign-born players in their team were Argentina, Brazil, South Korea and Saudi Arabia.

Soccer also came to a halt with the Covid-19 crisis. It has been completely paralyzed due to the pandemic. Local championships and international competitions were postponed indefinitely. Even the Tokyo Olympic Games, originally scheduled for June 2020, have been postponed until the following year.

---

6 Available at: https://www.transfermarkt.com/statistik/saisontransfers.

In a 30 March 2020 article in *O Estado de S. Paulo*, we get an idea of the size of the hole that the pandemic has caused to the European coffers of the ball world:

> The damage of the new coronavirus in soccer will go far beyond just paralyzing the championships. The predictions from financial experts are quite gloomy about how fragile the sport will become and undergo one of the biggest economic crises in history. The top five national leagues in Europe alone (England, Spain, Italy, Germany and France) may suffer an impact of the equivalent of R$ 20 billion if the championships cannot be resumed, according to a projection by consulting firm KPMG.[7]

As an example, it is also worth mentioning an article published in the same newspaper, on 6 May 2020. The article "Back in Wuhan, Brazilian forward describes climate in the landmark city of the coronavirus" mentions the local team of Wuhan in China, a local team that is in the elite league of the Chinese calendar. After 104 days away from Wuhan, the players and coaches returned to the city to resume training. He had left the city (epicenter of the global outbreak) initially for Guangzhou and then, as the virus spread in China, continued his pre-season in Sotogrande (Spain). However, after the disease arrived there, they decided to return to China and stayed in Shenzhen, where they were confined to a hotel for two weeks before a new lockdown.

The 2022 FIFA World Cup was held for the first time in November, to avoid the hot weather of June, when it is usually held. The investments made by the host country surpassed what other countries have invested so far. However, the organization of the world cup received great criticism due to the poor working conditions, including the number of deaths of workers while building the stadium. However, the games were held in a very smooth way and great attendance from all over the world. In the final game Argentina beat France to conquer its third world championship. The World Cup once again proved the importance of soccer as a global sport. The next World Cup, in June 2026, will be played for the first time in three different countries, United States, Canada and Mexico.

---

7 Pandemic is expected to cause losses of up to R$ 20 billion in European soccer. Available at: http://bit.ly/3pB68i2.

Chapter 17

ON THE AGENDA: THE AMAZON

One of Our Biggest Challenges

The reasons that make the Amazon forest important are superlative. This is the largest tropical forest in the world, contains the largest watershed on the planet and the largest amount of fresh water available on the globe. The biodiversity is impressive. "The Amazon represents the quintessence of bio-diversity—the richest ecosystem on Earth,"[1] according to the Smithsonian Institution in the United States. It is believed that the Amazon is home to between 10 and 20 percent of the world's known biodiversity. Based only at the rivers of the Amazon basin, it is estimated that they concentrate about 85 percent of the freshwater fish species in South America.

Claiming to want to direct special care to the region, politically, since the 1960s, the government has created the concept of the Legal Amazon. Representing about 60 percent of the national territory and presenting similar social and economic challenges throughout the nine states it covers, the "Legal Amazon" encompasses Acre, Amapá, Amazonas, Mato Grosso, Pará, Rondônia, Roraima and Tocantins and part of Maranhão. It constitutes an area of 5,217,423 km² of Brazilian territory, but, in population terms, it encompasses only 21 million inhabitants—12 percent of the population. It is interesting to note that more than 55 percent of the country's indigenous population, about 250,000 individuals, are concentrated in these states.[2]

But the forest is not restricted to the territorial limits of Brazil. The Hylean Amazon is multi-country. The jungle extends beyond Brazil to another eight South American countries. They are Bolivia, Colombia, Ecuador, France (French Guiana), Guyana, Peru, Suriname and Venezuela. It totals 7,413,827

---

1 Smithsonian Institution. Where Is the World's Greatest Biodiversity? Smithsonian Scientists Find the Answer Is a Question of Scale. *ScienceDaily*. Available at: http://bit .ly/2M5vzum. Accessed on: 22 Oct. 2019.
2 What Is the Legal Amazon. Environmental Dictionary. *((o))eco, Rio de Janeiro*, Nov. 2014. Available at: http://bit.ly/3s75ydy. Accessed on: 22 Oct. 2019.

km²! CONFUSO Because it is a forest that spawns multiple countries, the Amazon Cooperation Treaty Organization was created in 1978, while the Amazon Cooperation Treaty has existed since the late 1970s and has as its objective:[3]

> undertake joint efforts and actions to promote the harmonious development of their respective Amazonian territories, so that these joint actions produce equitable and mutually beneficial results in terms of environmental preservation and to the conservation and rational use of natural resources in these territories.[4]

The Amazon is fundamental for maintaining the world's climatic balance, and has a great influence on the transport of heat and water vapor to the regions located at higher latitudes. In addition, it plays a very important role in sequestering atmospheric carbon and, with this, contributes to the reduction of global warming.

Everything that is said about Amazon is immense, large, challenging, and often immeasurable. The challenges of the past and the future are imposed on us in the present. To work for the benefit of the region, it is indispensable to know its peculiarities and characteristics.

It accounts for more than half of the planet's tropical rainforest, and is the world's largest tropical rainforest. The region represents between 4 to 6% of the Earth's total surface, and between 25 to 40% of the surface of America. In addition, the Amazon region covers a surface area of 7,413,827 km², which represents 54% of the total surface area of the eight OTCA Member Countries: Brazil, Bolivia, Colombia, Ecuador, Guyana, Peru, Suriname and Venezuela.

The Amazon is also synonymous with cultural diversity, due to the fact that it is the result of a historical process of occupation of the territory and interaction between human groups of different ethnic and geographical origins.

The 34 million inhabitants account for 11% of the population of the eight Amazonian countries. There are 420 different indigenous and tribal peoples living there, speaking 86 languages and 650 dialects. Approximately 60 peoples live in total isolation. It is a region that has a large volume of natural wealth, fundamental for the economic and social development of its people.

---

3 For more information about the ACTO, see http://www.otca-oficial.info/.
4 *ACTO. Amazon Cooperation Treaty. Art. 1.*

The Amazon Fund (Fundo Amazonia) created in 2008 has, among other purposes, to supply funds to different indigenous groups and indigenists

The Amazon River has the largest hydrographic basin on the planet, and its rivers play an important role in the water cycle and water balance of the region.

The Amazon River rises in the Peruvian Andes at 5,597 meters above sea level and flows to its mouth in the Atlantic Ocean. The Amazon Basin contains approximately 20% of the planet's fresh water in the oceans. The Amazon River is 6,992 thousand kilometers long and is the largest in the world.

The Amazon has the highest water flow volume (220,000 m^3 per second) and carries more water than the Missouri-Mississippi, Nile, and Yangtze rivers combined.

The Amazon Water Cycle feeds a complex system of aquifers and groundwater, which can cover an area of almost 4 million km^2 between Brazil, Bolivia, Colombia, Ecuador, Peru, and Venezuela.

The Amazon is home to a great variety of species of flora and fauna, which has made it possible to establish world marks for biological diversity. It is also an important area of endemism, which makes it a genetic reserve of worldwide importance for the development of humanity.[5]

The Internationalization of the Amazon

In 2015, the United Nations Organization launched the so-called Sustainable Development Goals (SDGs), an action plan that brings together 17 goals and 169 targets that must be achieved by countries by the year 2030.

The plan, which is ambitious, addresses a wide range of issues. Hunger, agriculture, cities, marine environments, industry: several are the areas targeted by the goals set out in the so-called Agenda 2030.

The SDGs are based on the concept of sustainable development from the late 1980s. "Sustainable development is development that meets current needs without compromising the ability of future generations to meet their own needs," according to the 1987 report Our Common Future.[6]

---

5 *Our Amazon.* Available at: http://www.otca-oficial.info/amazon/our_amazon.
6 Available at: https://digitallibrary.un.org/record/139811?ln=en.

The idea is to reconcile economic growth with environmental preservation. In discourse it is inspiring, but implementation presents management difficulties. Overall, this is the biggest challenge that the world has faced in recent years.

Brazil has a great challenge in this regard. Cradle of the largest tropical forest in the world, the Amazon, owner of a huge territory and with a coastline that stretches for more than 7,000 kilometers, the country has difficulties on land, sea and air.

The issue of Amazonian internationalization was mentioned not only by some European countries like French president Macron, but recently by the newly elected president of Colombia, Gustavo Petro, reinforcing the importance of climate change and the relevance of Amazon forest. He also discussed the matter with the United States regarding drug control and a military unit was created with 12 helicopters to help combat drug traffickers and control forest fires. It represents a change where the United States is involved. The Colombian initiative should be looked upon cautiously due to strategic reasons, not only environmental but also defense policies.[7]

Amazonian Challenges

If the forest is superlative in its characterization, it is also superlative in terms of the challenges it faces. The list of problems is long, which shows the need to bring the strategic value of the region to the level of domestic priority.

At first, historically, the Amazon is one of the great reserves of tropical timber. It has been suffering an accelerated degradation process, due to predatory and illegal logging by clandestine logging companies. It has also suffered all kinds of environmental aggression, due to the predatory activities of miners (legal and illegal) in search of gold, polluting rivers and their affluents. Another problem is the expansive wave of agribusiness. The region also has development projects advancing along the rivers in the form of large hydroelectric dams.

Furthermore, the region has been the scene of innumerable episodes of illegal deforestation and fires, causing social conflicts, which clash with the interests of forest protection, demarcation of indigenous lands, agrarian and land reform.

In mid-2019, the Senate Environment Committee held public hearings to get further clarification on land grabbing and law enforcement in the

---

7 Availabe at: https://interessenacional.com.br/edicoes-posts/editorial-internacionali-zacao-da-amazonia/.

Amazon. For the president of the Commission, Senator Fabiano Contarato, surveillance, education and prevention are the pillars for the effective protection of the Amazon.

2019: The Year of the Amazon Crises

In the year 2019, deforestation, forest burning, lack of funds and inspectors were issues that gained national and international news. A reading that presidential policies would be more lenient and tolerant to offenders is also recalled to understand the current crisis that had great international repercussion, creating friction zones with some European countries, especially France.

NASA has indicated that 2019 was the worst year for fires in the Brazilian Amazon since 2010. The main focuses of fires are located on the edges of highways. For scientists, the burning activity in the Amazon forest from year to year, from month to month, has been influenced by economic and climatic changes.

The U.S. Agency, however, found that although drought played an important role in intensifying the fires, larger than at other times, the number and location of fires detected at the start of the driest season of 2019 seem linked more to deforestation than to seasonal drought.

This is not the first time, and most likely will not be the last, that the Amazon issue leaves the domestic news and becomes relevant worldwide. In early 2020, for example, the World Economic Forum released the Global Risks Report 2020, in which there was no shortage of warnings to the Brazilian government about the Amazon.

> The document states that the abrupt loss of Amazon cover could have an economic cost of $3 trillion. [...] In the same section that deals with the Amazon, the report highlights risks for agricultural markets, remembering that Brazil is one of the largest exporters of commodities such as soy, corn, and meat.[8]

The report, which is based on the opinions of 750 experts, casts doubt on the future of the food market and the insecurity that this can generate, as well as warning about the damage to the indigenous communities that depend on the Amazon territory.

---

8 Losses in the Amazon Can Exceed US$ 3 tri. *O Globo, Rio de Janeiro*, 16 Jan. 2020.

A study done by the renowned Fundação Getulio Vargas has estimated that losses caused by deforestation increased in the last years. The study, released by *O Globo* on 19 October 2022, indicates that between 2019 and 2022 it generated economic losses of R$ 1.18 trillion, representing US$ 229 billion or 12.3 percent of our GDP.

It also indicates that we are having the worst deforestation rates since 2003.

From 2019 to 2022, the destruction of the forest will probably reach 49.000 km² or a 72 percent increase compared to 2015/2018.

One explanation for this substantial increase is the lack of enforcement, as Bolsonaro reduced the budget for that purpose.

The Amazon Is Ours!

The topic of "sovereignty" has come up again, with the untimely mention, albeit indirectly, of President Macron, who brought up the topic of our sovereignty over the region.

The issue of the environment and its consequences on climate behavior with respect to global warming and the Amazon rainforest are back in the headlines, putting us in a defensive position.

Under all aspects, the incontestable fact is that the Brazilian elites—and in them are included not only the business classes, but above all those who have a prominent position in society, including the political class—have not been giving the Amazon theme the attention and prominence it deserves in discussions about public policy priorities.

We must include the Amazon issue in the National Strategy for the Defense of our territory as a clearly defined land policy, marking a greater presence in the region, so that the issue of indigenous lands is visible and respected, as well as the possibilities of exploiting the mineral wealth that exists there should be made explicit, in an open and transparent way. It should also be noted that it has been the object of presidential statements to respect indigenous rights.

Only in moments of crisis do we realize its relevance for our country and how we need to pay more attention to it and resources to avoid that possible questions regarding our autonomy over the region could be brought into the discussion and lead to unnecessary and inappropriate tension.

Attempts to challenge national sovereignty over the forest are not new. History shows some episodes, as reported in the text *Internacionalização da Amazônia* by Almir Pazzianotto Pinto, lawyer, former minister of Labor and former president of the Superior Labor Court, 27 September 2019:

> The first concrete attempt at foreign penetration in the region occurred in the second half of the 19th century, when the American government

learned of a project developed by the Bolivian government to build a railroad to export rubber across the Atlantic Ocean.

The incorporation of Acre under the Treaty of Petrópolis, negotiated by Rio Banco, cost us 2 million pounds sterling and the construction of the 366-kilometer Madeira-Mamoré Railroad.

[...]

[...] Already in the early 1920s, Henry Ford considered becoming self-sufficient in the production of tires for the automobiles produced in Detroit. For this purpose, he acquired a vast area on the banks of the Tapajós River, where he built a village with all the conveniences of the time, set up a rubber factory, planted 3 million rubber trees, and hired 2,700 employees.

[...] In the 1960s, the pulp business attracted American Daniel Keith Ludwig, a billionaire connected to the shipping sector, to the Rio Jari region In March 1967, Ludwig concluded negotiations with the government of President Castelo Branco to found the Jari Florestal e Agropecuária company, part of the Jari Indústria e Comércio S/A group. The project aimed to produce pulp, explore kaolin deposits, cultivate corn, cassava and rice, raise cattle to raise cattle, in an area of 1,632,121 hectares, of which 1,174,391 hectares are in the municipality of Almeirim (Pará) and 457,730 hectares in the then Federal Territory of Amapá, municipality of Mazagão.[9]

Reality Shocks

The naked truth is that we have an infrastructure that is incompatible with reality, in total deficiency of public security, sanitation and lack of qualified labor. The state has not complied with its constitutional obligations, either because of a lack of resources or because it is not giving priority, in the national strategy, to the indigenous people.

Visits by different political and business groups have not happened often and with clearly defined goals. In addition, the population density is also far below national standards, and those who live there are not achieving a satisfactory standard of living. In addition, widespread ignorance about the Amazon is prevalent in the general population.

The defense system leaves much to be desired, and our Armed Forces, particularly the Army, are struggling to do the bare minimum compatible with our responsibility. Other federal agencies have also been present, but

---

9 Available at: http://bit.ly/2OJ4P3J. Accessed on: 2 Nov. 2019.

their commitment to the tasks assigned to them has not had the desirable commitment.

Another problem to be addressed is that of NGOs. Their number is not yet clearly counted, and their objectives are partially defined. The participation of NGOs with foreign funds would also need to be better identified. And there is the suspicion that some simply exist for surveys of reserves of medicinal and other herbal products that are there to be exploited, and not for the noble purposes for which they were created.

Another point is to revitalize our projects in harmony with our neighbors, clearly defining each other's rights and responsibilities. In this regard, it is little publicized that OTCA met to discuss the steps to be taken regarding the Amazon fires in early September 2019.

Obviously, the issue of education once again comes to the scene. It should receive greater attention and thereby open up greater opportunities for those who live there.

If there is passivity, we will certainly be running the imminent risk of becoming a haven for illicit behavior.

As a natural consequence, the issue of drug trafficking control arises: the Amazon could become a frontier for the proliferation of drug traffickers, in a smuggling party. We have flows of different types of drugs (cocaine, crack and other heavier drugs) by land, sea and river and with all the associated banditry. There is a risk that this illicit behavior will escalate if it is not properly policed and controlled.

This clearly demonstrates our difficulties in having effective border control and certainly demonstrates a major national security challenge.

Last but not least, the presence of different religious groups should be mentioned. Most of them have the purpose of evangelization, giving hope to the inhabitants of the region. There are, however, other religions suspected to be in the region with other intentions not explicitly defined, more interested in what lies underground.

Another field to attack is to find common ground between "ruralistas" and environmentalists, to develop peaceful coexistence, respecting the interests of the environment and existing regulations.

Amazonian issues should be emphasized as a national priority from the school benches on. Its importance and connection to the environmental issue should also be addressed by company leaders and experts in business schools, as it involves risk analysis as an element of corporate governance.

In 2021, the National Institute for Space Research (INPE) registered 75.090 fires. Unfortunately in 2022 (jan/Sep) it reached 76.587 fires, overcoming the previous year.[10] However, the environmental policies implemented by Bolsonaro's government were very far from mending this problem.

The newspapers reported that on 3 June the vice president, Hamilton Mourão, in a lecture at FIESP, presented the work plan National Council of the Legal Amazon (Conselho Nacional da Amazônia Legal), in search of measures to create a positive image of Brazil "as a country that is committed to the international principles of environmental protection, ensure the presence of the state in all corners of the Amazon and use, in a sustainable way, the natural resources that exist in the region, while promoting the social inclusion of the local population."[11] In addition, he commented on the federal government's articulation in the Amazon Fund in relation to its main funders, among which are Germans and Norwegians.

The general, on 9 July 2020, summoned managers of investment and pension funds, domestic and international, as well as some from the government, to address the issue of deforestation in the Amazon. He also addressed the regression in our environmental policy. It is a reaction not only to the managers of large international investments that, in a manifestation, expressed their dissatisfaction with the current environmental policy and warned that they saw the current government as a strong impediment to invest in the country.

Likewise, this unprecedented action was followed by a representative group of former finance ministers and Central Bank presidents, who signed a public document in which they expressed their concern to the current government, affirming the need for constructive attitudes regarding environmental policy that deals with the issue of Amazonian fires and deforestation.

Within the same context, on 22 July 2022, three of the largest private banks in the country (Bradesco, Itaú and Santander) launched a plan for sustainable development in the Amazon, having been signatories of a document sent to General Hamilton Mourão, president of the Amazon Council. The initiative covers conservation, infrastructure and guaranteeing the rights of the population. Several measures are considered priorities: environmental conservation and stimulation of the bio-economy, investment in sustainable infrastructure and guarantee of basic rights for the population, valorization of the Amazon and its natural wealth, favoring biodiversity.

---

10 Available at: http://bit.ly/3u8pONE.
11 Available at: https://bit.ly/3axQVdo.

A few months later, in December, the three banks detailed the initiative, making available almost R$ 4.8 trillion of their own resources to finance productive chains in the region, amid demands for a more assertive position of the Bolsonaro government in environmental preservation and response to international demands.

I am among those who truly believe that the Amazon theme will gradually occupy a commensurate space on the governmental and private sector agendas.

Certainly, investors, corporations and individual took initiatives to protect Amazonian region and certainly that will be an important tool to fight deforestation and aggressive participation of smugglers that infest the region.

Concluding, Amazonia is an open page, and the countries of the region should prioritize in their policies the repression of illegal activities, especially deforestation and drug traffic. If that is not done, the risk of external intervention will increase and will become part of the international agenda.

While attending COP 27 in Sharm El-Sheikh, Egypt, Lula presented a long and sensible speech where he made clear that the Amazon will be one of the main issues during his third term.

He suggested that the next COP, to be held in 2025, should take place in the state of Amazonas.

Part 6

IN A WORLD IN TRANSITION, HOW WILL GEOPOLITICS AFFECT BRAZIL?

Chapter 18

CONCLUDING REMARKS

After so much discourse, a simple but direct and objective question remains: So what? I would start by answering this question with the presentation I made in Cartagena, Colombia, in 1996, perhaps in one of the most important events I have attended as president of the Latin American Business Council (Ceal).

At that event, I well remember that at the table were then U.S. secretary of Commerce Ron Brown (who later died in a plane crash) and Thomas "Mack" McLarty, then president Clinton's special envoy to the Americas. It was a meeting that brought together the Foreign Trade Ministers of the region and was preceded by the Americas Business Forum. I remember a phrase that I registered on that occasion: "who does not make dust eats dust"! McLarty always refers to this expression in our conversations!

In the text I presented at the time, I drew attention to the substantial increase in Brazil's trade flows with the Mercosur countries at the time. Even considering the effects of the pandemic, I believe they are still relevant:

1. Expansion of trade at the regional level that would have to be consistent with the multilateral system at the global level, maximizing the benefits of further integration.
2. Governments should provide the political conditions, with the definition of structures that value these objectives. The issue of infrastructure is always remembered.
3. It is crucial that the degree of predictability increases: advances followed by setbacks cause perplexity and uncertainty.
4. Pursue greater facilities with a continuous flow of investments.

I called attention to the growing investment of Brazilian companies abroad, which became known as "Multilatinas," to seek their expansion in a global market. In the past only engineering companies such as Odebrecht, Andrade Gutierrez, Mender Jr. were contractors of large works and were pioneers in obtaining important contracts abroad; however, they were also the victims or perpetrators for the ethical deviations uncovered by Lava Jato.

I registered that Embraco (then controlled by the Brasmotor Group) was one of the pioneers in establishing itself in China, with a compressor factory in Beijing in association with Chinese capital. Companhia Brasileira de Metalurgia e Mineração, which produces an iron–niobium alloy, signed pioneering contracts with Russia and China in 1977/1978. Other traditional groups, such as Votorantim, Gerdau, Vale, CSN and Weg, began to mark their activities with important investments abroad.

Some of the factors that drove such companies overseas were as follows:

- Attractive asset prices associated with a favorable exchange rate;
- Unfavorable infrastructure in our country that stimulated investment abroad;
- The scale of the global market;
- Improved competitiveness and more modern technologies, including adding greater value to their export products;
- It was also the beginning of the process in which the BNDES encouraged going abroad;
- Finally, I pointed out that in the well-known case of Ambev (the merger of Antarctica and Brahma) there was an important movement of Brazilian professionals assuming positions in the parent company abroad.

In 2014, in an article for *Valor Econômico* newspaper, I warned that "internationalization was a path with no return," and that of the 15 largest economies in the world, the degree of internationalization of the Brazilian economy in world trade was among the lowest. Finally I commented on the negative fact of taxation on the profits of Brazilian multinationals, a factor that slowed down our international insertion, as we verified in the answers to the questionnaires we sent to Brazilian companies with important investments abroad. It remains a worrisome problem for our entrepreneurs.

In a document dated 21 November 1995, from the Aspen Institute, I transcribed what had been my experience as a participant, in April of that year, during five days in Great Exuma, in the Bahamas, where I participated in the so-called Congressional Program, to discuss the situation of Brazil in relation to the United States. The participants, for the most part, were Democratic congressmen. To counterbalance my presence as the only Brazilian, five Brazilianists were invited, two of them very well known: Monica Hirst and Riordan Roett. The 15 legislators were without advisors and were addressed by first name. Total informality (no cell phones).

I was not surprised that right at the opening it was evident, regardless of the material distributed, that there was misinformation about our country, which, in the end, led me to the conclusion that the private sector in total agreement with Brazilian authorities needed to design a program of continuous discussion with the U.S. Congress, to better understand our problems in the trade area and to have a greater identity in the challenges faced in a democratic government.

That is a goal we must continue to pursue since it is of paramount importance.

The FTAA was one of the topics under discussion (which would have been a free trade agreement between all countries in the Americas) that did not advance, with each side placing the responsibility on the other. I have never had any doubt that the U.S. Congress was unlikely to rectify an agreement with Brazil, probably stipulating conditions that would not be acceptable to us.

In a text from 2005, I referred to what I called the "Business Decalogue." Many years have passed, but I believe that to this day, many of the issues I raised at the time remain valid, despite Covid-19. I present them in the following:

I. Let's start with the obvious: It is necessary to master foreign languages, whether it's English (the language used in international business) or German, French or Italian. It is essential to speak Spanish well, and not the "portunhol" that we mostly improvise.

II. University or even professional courses should devote more and more space to issues related to international trade or, more broadly, to international relations. The interest in the field of International Relations is encouraging which today is part of the options that Brazilian students find in the undergraduate programs of the largest Brazilian universities. There should be an incentive for companies to open up opportunities for recent graduates, thus giving them the chance to work in their chosen field;

III. Companies must continue to make a great effort in the area of quality and costs control in order to be internationally competitive. There is no doubt that we have made great progress in recent years, but the reality is that developed economies have had superior productivity gains. Digitalization and IT will play a fundamental role.

The diversity and location of our country, far from the major markets, forces us to a level of competitiveness and productivity gains that can minimize this distance. Therefore, the logistics issue, the ports issue, isonomies and capital cost are matters of the utmost relevance.

IV. The Boards of Directors of companies with export potential should have a strategic vision of international insertion and a permanent follow-up of the external area. Without this commitment, the companies will hardly have a strong presence abroad. There is no longer any way of intransigently defending the internal market, because many markets are integrated. Although the production chains have been affected and criticized for their high dependence on one supplier, still some degree of integration will always exist. On the other hand, the multinational companies installed here should collaborate in the export effort, including with products of higher added value, expanding our export agenda.

V. Companies with export potential need to continue investing in the training of technicians versed in matters relating to international relations. In meetings with professionals from foreign companies operating in the sector, the quality of their knowledge and business training is transparent. The training must include technicians and employees dedicated to the export area in courses, seminars and events that enhance their knowledge. Internships abroad would be extremely productive in this training process. It is worth nothing that even employees who already come from International Relations courses still lack practical experience in the career, since degrees in the area tend to focus primarily on theory.

VI. Attendance at international meetings and forums is essential. Traveling is necessary. Without this attendance, the chief executive will hardly feel the atmosphere, the external environment and establish the relationships that will be important for his activities. In the meetings I have attended, the top executives of multinational companies mark their presence, accompanied by excellent advisors.

Now, with the spread of webinars, the need to travel to participate in international seminars has been greatly reduced. It is an alternative, although I recognize that personal contacts are relevant in these events.

VII. It is essential to have a common, postulated agenda. Thus, preparatory meetings are fundamental for the alignment of positions and dialogue with government sectors that are involved with the sector. This is not to suggest that unanimity should be sought, or that individual interests should not be considered. We must not, however, abuse our well-known ability to improvise.

VIII. The industry associations need to continuously equip themselves with the informational and human material capable of putting us at a level compatible with our international counterparts. Participation needs to increase. Just look at the process of this survey: although the question-naire was sent to about twenty class entities from different industrial sectors, only two were willing to answer it. We can interpret this low response rate as a lack of interest from its members regarding interna-tional insertion. In these entities, it would be interesting to invite those who have had experience in the foreign market to share their experi-ence with the other members.

The exchange of experiences between companies that have already gone abroad should be encouraged, not only among themselves but also with others that are considering this possibility. This exchange of experiences will certainly bring gains for everyone, increasing our competitiveness and efficiency of a greater presence abroad.

Since we know that human and material resources are scarce, we must not, for this very reason, disperse them. In this way, following the example of entrepreneurs in other countries, we could concentrate on a well-structured organization, to which all the others would be linked, our capacity for negotiation in foreign trade, to which all those with connections in the sector would be integrated. As an example: the Indian National Confederation of Industry maintains offices in several major capitals around the world, including Washington.

In this sense, it is fundamental for Congress to have greater involvement in the issue of foreign relations. The Foreign Affairs Committees, in particular, should be streamlined, with their counsel preparing information material, with the purpose of spreading knowl-edge to laymen or to those who already have *expertise* and seek con-tinuous improvement and frequent dialogue with Itamaraty. Periodic meetings with the private sector are recommended.

IX. It is important to understand the transcendence of free trade agree-ments and customs unions, such as Mercosur. We are stronger when we present ourselves as a bloc, since the developed countries are increasingly organized in the form of economic blocs, or else they act as real steamrollers. Toward our neighbors, to be patient, to under-stand and to help them in solving problems with which, as partners, we are necessarily involved.

So we must not neglect to meet, as far as possible, the needs of our Mercosur partners. There is bitterness, particularly from Paraguayans and Uruguayans, who feel ignored by the Brazilian authorities and businessmen, highlighting the asymmetries that exist in the same commercial relationship.

X. In the new world economy it is essential to implement cooperation with all authorities involved in the international arena. You have to participate! It is necessary to seek constructive collaboration and provide answers when requested in a timely manner. We must put aside ideological aspects and look at common interests in the short–medium–long term, as well as know what we want and have a more offensive posture. A compatible structure of the different sectors involved is fundamental. More than ever, we are obliged to take a position of the role we should play.

I pointed, back in 2004, to an aspect that I still consider pertinent, that is, at that time, the "opening" of the Brazilian market, made during the government of President Fernando Collor de Mello, criticized for having opened our economy (albeit in a relatively small scale), without having asked for anything in return. I do not join those who think this way. I also remember a phrase that I recorded in a lecture: "We are very vocal in what we don't want, but we can't consensually define what we do want."

I cite such a phrase in this text because I believe that for the first time the expression "Business Diplomacy" was decisive when our Argentine neighbors complained bitterly, and the exchange rate measures taken by the Brazilian government affected the trade flow between our two countries. The businessmen had to intervene, in order to calm down the tempers and ended up acting as legitimate diplomats.

We lacked the perception (which many still do not accept) that in a relationship with Mercosur, trade and investment relations have to be managed in order to avoid that one of the parties is always at a commercial disadvantage in relation to its stronger partner and that instruments should be sought to mitigate this discomfort.

Finally I commented on the Permanent Business Committee (CEP), created during Luiz Felipe Lampreia's term at the head of the Ministry of Foreign Affairs with the objective of bringing businessmen together to share a long-term strategic vision with the managers of our foreign policy. Later on, these meetings got smaller and became about many specific rather than strategic interests. It was later discontinued, a priceless loss.

I note, finally, the performance of then president Lula on the international scene. Succeeding President Fernando Henrique Cardoso, who had marked his eight years in office with a strong international presence, President Lula also had an outstanding participation at different times, and hit the road and was instrumental in creating the G20, the South–South Dialogue, strengthening institutional political ties with South American countries and even with the controversial decision to grant market economy status to China, which has not materialized to this day.

The performance of the two presidents, under the geopolitical point of view, was positive and we managed, during this period, to gradually change our image abroad. The recognition of Brazil as an emerging power has happened, even though from the point of view of external convergence and greater presence as an exporter of manufactures, we have not had appreciable changes.

Foreign policy for the internationalization of the country must be a permanent state strategy, not a positioning strategy, according to the government of the day!

I think that in every respect the fact that I had to revise my text in light of the events caused by the Covid-19 pandemic had a positive aspect. I was forced to look at the future in a different way. Even with a level of great uncertainty that prevailed in the first half of 2020, still, and I believe that we are going to have perceptible changes in the behavior of our societies, whether in terms of our social coexistence or even in terms of our relationship with the outside world.

In an interview with the *Financial Times* on 8 July 2020, the president of the European Central Bank, Christine Lagarde, noted that the pandemic is having a brutal impact, in the worst market recession in European countries since the end of World War II. She stated that the whole set of relations and market of the countries will have to be reviewed.[1]

What will be the "new normal" was not at all clear as I was writing these lines. However, if there is any consensus, with so many uncertainties in the air, it is that we will be very far from being able to live with a stable and predictable scenario in the short term. There are few certainties and many doubts that only time will help us clarify.

Unfortunately, some of the problems that we have historically seen in our country and also in the rest of the world will continue to be evident. We give, as an example, a central theme that is the social issue of income distribution, and nothing makes us believe that we can have positive changes in the short term. On the contrary, the damage done to the economy and businesses will take some time to overcome the imbalances created. In our specific case, the deficiencies in the educational sector, health care, basic sanitation and urban planning were also evident. In other words, the deficiencies that existed, and with which we have become accustomed to neglect, have now become transparent and require not only the current government, but future ones as well, to seek lasting solutions as a matter of priority. Some of them will have to be state policies, not policies of a government. When we talk about government,

---

1 Available at: http://on.ft.com/3azOyGU.

we should not limit ourselves to the Presidency of the Republic, but also to the legislative and judiciary branches.

In many cases, from lived experience, our elites and society in general have let slip the feeling that time is in our favor. We don't realize that, on the contrary, we are far behind and sleeping in a cradle that has nothing splendid about it.

Therefore, the sense of urgency must be considered. We have to hurry, and we can't afford to waste any more time. The concern to serve different publics, some of them defended by vested interests that exert strong pressure against change, has slowed down. These various reforms cannot serve as a pretext or an impediment to reforms moving forward, regardless of ideological views.

In this context, our insertion in the world must be among our top priorities and we cannot be afraid of the world! Therefore, active participation in the global arena is fundamental.

We cannot continue to be mere spectators internationally and must be important players. This is a collective effort that all of society has to be involved in, and we have to be connected, and with this, create a new image of Brazil abroad, I repeat, what I have registered in different moments throughout the text. Our image is not created from the outside in, but quite the opposite. What we talk about and register with those who visit us, the same ones who read about it, will resonate out there. We cannot close our eyes to the problems, but we must have confidence in our ability to be resilient.

Yes, there are enormous problems and incredible challenges that will take many years to solve. However, this should not be an excuse for us to shrink back and cultivate our wounds. We can't stop looking with a critical eye, but we can list what is positive about us and what we have already done. Never forget that we are aware of our problems and the need to solve them.

Therefore, losing fear is fundamental when dealing with the crisis in the country and facing the increasing challenges, within a universe in an accelerated transformation process. Could this crisis not bring us opportunities to better position ourselves in the world context? As we look around the world, who doesn't have challenges to face? We're not the ugly duckling.

Therefore, it is fundamental to look with confidence at our potential to occupy a place compatible with its people and its continental size and countless resources in the world context.

AFTERWORD—POST-PANDEMIC: WHAT IS IN STORE?

The future of the world is unknown. There are many guesses, but only time will tell who was right in prospecting the world's socioeconomic structure. Everything indicates, however, that a brave new world is nothing but a utopia!

Quite the contrary! Analyses made at the time of the pandemic indicated, that, unfortunately, inequalities were widening and the number of people living below the poverty level was increasing, at the same time that resources for emergency support were running out.

In an interview given to *Valor* newspaper on 16 April 2020, Chinese economist Andy Chie, PhD in Economics from the Massachusetts Institute of Technology, who has worked for the IMF and Morgan Stanley as the head of Asia/Pacific, when asked about the end of globalization, said: "I think globalization, the way it was, is over." Basically, chains and supply for cost minimization are fragile and vulnerable. Governments will want factories capable of producing for the country, even without making a profit. There will be an effort and policy to maintain some productive capacity domestically, as we noted in the introductory text.

Pierre Salama, professor emeritus at the University of Paris, is convinced that the days of a system of globalization as practiced until now are over. The economic model of the last decades, which was already showing signs of a certain exhaustion, would be collapsing because of a virus and the war in Ukraine. He compared it to the crisis of 1929, considering it to be of a smaller size. He suggested rethinking the economy in its human relations between the state and the market (*O Globo*, 14 April 2020). He also said that we are seeing the end of a cycle of capitalism! It will no longer be what it was in the past.

Several international analysts, from different countries, stated that they expect changes in the global supply chain, not only in its geographical distribution. Identifying this vulnerability should also change the way industries operate. For some countries, the lesson learned has caused some industries to seek to diversify their suppliers, or even to obtain, as an alternative, metal recycling. Japan has given indications that it will create incentives for the local production of imported inputs. Moreover, the war in Ukraine and the sanctions against Russia are going to have a deep impact in the supply chain, particularly in area of oil and gas as well as in fertilizers.

The World Will No Longer Be the Same?

The newspaper *O Globo*, on 13 April 2020, in an article about the Virus of the Revolution, referring to Covid-19 consequences in different areas, summarized the thoughts of six personalities, as follows:

a. "People will rely more on science to make decisions"—Mozart Neves Ramos, holder of the Sérgio Henrique Ferreira Chair at the Institute of Advanced Studies at USP-Ribeirão Preto;
b. "Without SUS, (Brazilian system of public health) we would be much worse off today"—Lígia Bahia, public health physician and professor at UFRJ (Federal University of Rio de Janeiro);
c. "Every crisis also opens a crack"—Lilia Schwarcz, historian and anthropologist, professor at USP and Princeton;
d. "May the pain of now be the cure tomorrow"—Luiz Antônio Simas, writer and history professor;
e. "It is possible to stop, to decrease the consumption, the devastation"— Christian Dunker, psychoanalyst and professor at the Psychology Institute at USP.

It is difficult to question such reasoning, and in some cases we may say that the future divides opinions. For the literary critic and writer Silviano Santiago, in an interview to *Folha de S.Paulo*, optimism prevails. "By the chance of the pandemic one knows best the capacity for rupture and renewal and human invention. Each narrow universe of participants in the vital experience of surviving gets wider and wider. We will survive in a happier, more just and equal society."

The great Argentine conductor Daniel Barenboim, who completed 80 years in November 2022, on the other hand, takes a more somber view of the changes to come. Change forever? Caring for others and helping those who need it most? He answers: "frankly, I don't believe in that very much. The instinct to do things for good is a wonderful instinct, but it doesn't last. Hate, and everything negative, is much more exciting than good."

Also, for completeness, personality statements that do not necessarily share the majority's thinking (or who think outside the box), I would like to quote the philosopher Franco "Bifo" Berardi. He said, in an interview to *O Globo*, on 13 April 2020, that the recession caused by the epidemic can inspire more egalitarian social arrangements and suggests that the main political battle of the new century will not be between right and left, but between humans and inhuman transhumans. "'Inhuman transhumans' are those who exploit new technologies to create a techno-totalitarian system," he explains. Continuing the interview:

> The concept of a virus was used by William Burroughs (American writer, 1914–1997) to define everything that induces a mutation, be it cultural, linguistic or social. A third of the world's population is quarantined, everything is paralyzed, production, social interactions, air traffic, urban life. To understand what is happening, we have to take into account the psychological mutation that the virus has produced and its social effects in the near future.

He ended by leaving a disturbing question: "The future is so bleak that it terrifies us to imagine what is to come. The unpredictable is inevitable."

An important consideration was made by Yuval Harari, one of today's best-known philosophers and author of best sellers such as *Sapiens*, *Homo Deus* and *21 Lessons for the 21st Century*, in a long interview with Luciano Huck, published in *O Estado de S. Paulo*, on 12 April 2020.

"In recent years, cooperation between countries has weakened, and now we are paying the price. I hope it is not too late to reverse course. Likewise, if you think simply about the economic situation, now is the time for international organizations like the IMF and the World Bank, allied with the richest countries, to create a global safety net to ensure that no country falls into complete economic chaos (what we saw until April 2020 was that each country was trying to solve its own problems). Basically, that was Henry Kissinger's position, presented in the beginning of the pandemic."

He acknowledged mistakes, slowness, weaknesses in logistics and useless procedures in the fight against the coronavirus. He finished, in the same vein as other personalities: "There is a chance in this crisis to come together and prove our humility, to build another project in understanding, a reason to live deeply." A fine example he has set, not shying away from his mistakes, and looking forward to change. This is not what we have seen in many other countries, nor have we heard from world leaders who have sought as an excuse to accuse others, within their own countries and in other countries. Unfortunately, we were no exception!

Changes in Sight: Our Central Theme!

In the following we will record some of the very possible consequences of the global crisis caused by Covid-19, as far as international relations are concerned, mainly seeking to reflect how the crisis alters our relationship with the outside world. Such considerations, or at least part of them, were aggravated by the war in Ukraine

I. Supply chains

Companies are rethinking global chains. There may be a shift in globalization in this respect. The previous events of heavy dependence on medical/hospital supplies from China have created local problems and have stimulated supplier diversification and favored local producers. They will have an impact on costs because of the issue of scale of production. "Just in time" will be at risk and companies will work with larger inventories in order not to risk having to stop production due to lack of components.

The relationship between the United States and China tends to be a major factor in supply chains, given the relevance of these countries in the supply of industrial products and components. It was estimated that world trade may drop by up to 30 percent, significantly affecting the price of domestic and global commodities.

II. Remote working

Experiments with remote work, or telecommuting, which have already been happening, will be accelerated because it will be realized that many jobs can be performed outside the office, with the exception only of essential functions that require the physical presence of employees.

However, in 2022, the situation was not the same and an equilibrium was reached in most cases where personal contacts were relevant and, in some cases, essential. Before the requirement of social isolation, 15.2 percent of employees in Brazil telecommuted. Today it is 50 percent. In an article in the same newspaper, it was also indicated that the judges of different courts are being more productive working from home in the analysis and decision of cases.

In some companies, remote work has come to stay but in most of them, there will be a hybrid model.

We consider that, despite the shake-up, office life will not end. Personal contact, after all, has never been more valued than during Covid-19. To be seen! This relationship between people is a hallmark of civilization and should not disappear. But, no doubt, remote work will also facilitate the use of human resources from abroad!

III. Change in habits and international repercussions

A by-product of changes in these consumption habits may benefit products that are environmentally friendly and nonpolluting, as we will see later. I believe in a society that will increase the awareness of its duties and obligations. Without such a concept of citizenship, it will be difficult to accomplish sensible environmental changes.

Finally, I would mention that the home delivery system, which was fundamental for the survival of certain activities (particularly restaurants) which has already been expanding, will consolidate not only in the food business, but also, for example, purchases in supermarkets, drugstores, which already had a relevant participation in the segment of electro-electronic products, cell phones, etc. This implies the valorization of the work of the motorcycle couriers and delivery companies. Probably, in due time that services will require some regulation.

Therefore, so-called e-commerce, taking advantage of the closing of stores, will continue to increase its share of the consumer market, even after the end of the so-called new normal.

This position is not shared unanimously. Some analysts believe that once the crisis is over, consumers will return to their old patterns that in some regions are already happening.

IV. Capital markets

Foreign investors have significantly reduced their participation in the primary and secondary markets. Until the end of May 2022, foreigners had maintained a bearish attitude toward the market, even with abundant global liquidity. In the second half of the year, they cautiously returned to the market. But the war in Ukraine and the better results for Brazilian economy forecasted for 2022 have created a positive mood for foreign portfolio investors.

Exchange-traded stocks initially suffered sharp declines, whether traditional stocks or those that had been offered to the market in 2019. However, the reaction of the external markets, especially the New York Stock Exchange, in the months following the start of the pandemic, and the inflow of resources by different countries to mitigate the effects of the crisis on the economic plan have slowed down the initial losses in the stock market indices. Surprisingly, if we analyze the indexes from January to October

(Dow Jones, Standard & Poor's, Ibovespa) it is possible to observe a degree of resilience. Market projections are much dependent on world growth in different regions

The behavior of stock prices at the NYSE will certainly have a great influence on the international markets, as we have seen in other periods.

The ESG agenda should also have to be considered in the process of showing that companies going to market are aware of their responsibilities, as indeed major global investors had been making clear in their policies and pronouncements, since 2019. It will be increasingly present in the decisions of investors, especially multinationals that are fundamentally exposed to the climate issue.

V. Greater state participation

It will grow again! It is clear that the state will have more information about its citizens. Gabriela Zanfir-Fortuna, counselor of the NGO Future of Privacy Forum, in an interview to *Folha de S.Paulo* on 19 April 2020, commented that fighting Covid-19 will create "a society tracked like never before." Historically, in critical moments like the present, exceptional measures are accepted and there are excesses. The riskiest thing is that after the pandemic there is no retreat in the degree of monitoring.

Some observers properly comment that one of the worst consequences of the war in Ukraine will be that G7 and G20 will not have the chance to effectively discuss what will be accomplished in the climate, discussions that depend mostly of an agreement between leading countries. A consensus is mandatory to reach tangible results.

In the event of another major climate disaster, as occurred in 2019 and 2020 with the Amazon wildfires, it will remain in the headlines. It is crucial that we do not lose sensitivity about this issue and that we do not leave it relegated to the back burner, since the new U.S. government has made clear its displeasure with the fires in the Amazon.

Therefore, the state should not ease its commitments to environmental protection once the pandemic crisis is over.

Democracy will be strongly affected by the crisis, which has created a pretext for strong state intervention in the economy, something that has already happened in some countries where populists have gained ground in recent elections (Italy is typical).

Surveys made by the deputy director of V-Dem (Sweden's Institute for Variations in Democracy), Anna Lührmann, concluded that at the end of March 2020, 92 countries had authoritarian regimes and 87 democratic ones, with our country ranking the lowest in the world in the concept of a full democracy. Certainly, strong state intervention to mitigate the negative effects of the coronavirus will take time for a return to the previous status.

VI. Migration issue

Possible consequences of Brazilians living abroad are, in first place, the number of existing opportunities. Many Brazilians who migrated to Portugal are trying to return due to the lack of jobs and high cost of living.

Another consequence is that immigrants will face greater difficulties (some insurmountable) in finding shelter in many countries. Border controls will be stricter, as is the case with Venezuelans in Roraima and even, in some cases, with permanent border closures.

In an article published by *Folha* on 8 May 2020, Claudia Costin, with extensive experience in the field of education, mentioned the stories concerning education when referring to Venezuelan refugees, recalling that different surveys indicated that hardly anyone, with lower skills in their home country, wish to go on adventures to leave their country to earn a little more. As she aptly points out, during crises, placing the immigrant as the main culprit for the ills that afflict us makes no sense.

In a webinar in early May to discuss educational responses to the pandemic, the education secretary in Boa Vista (Roraima), speaking of the municipal school system's efforts with the adoption of remote emergency learning for the city's students, when asked if Venezuelans were being assisted, made it clear that: "Naturally, after all they are our students." A fine example of citizenship!

VII. International relations in disarray and the emergence of a new Cold War?

Some questions must be considered regarding the future of the relationship between states.

First of all, there is the issue of international coordination (or lack of it). During the pandemic, what we saw was disappointing: every man for himself. Great leaders have questioned isolation, but what we have witnessed is a lack of predictability and a power vacuum. Most countries acted in isolation and were unprepared to face a crisis of a transnational nature. However, the way to improve the situation seems to be through cooperation.

In fact, the Covid-19 factor and the way in which Trump handled the pandemic are considered to be the main reasons for Biden's victory in the November 2020 election.

Standing out in this power vacuum scenario is the United States, the superpower. The country proved to be unprepared for the pandemic, with the highest number of deaths in the world. It is also worth noting the strong dependence on imported supplies, mainly from Asia, China and Japan. About 25 percent of the world's production of ventilated respirators and masks is concentrated in China, as are test supplies.

The lack of cooperation could be seen in the attempts to reconcile health solutions, fundamental to combating Covid-19 but clearly unpopular, with electoral goals, as in the case of Trump and Bolsonaro, among others. Worldwide, this "dispute" has taken on the false dilemma of protecting public health or the economy. As if there were a tradeoff.

In addition to the lack of cooperation, during more difficult moments of the crisis a hardening of relations between China and the United States was observed.

Since 2018, we have seen an escalation of tensions in the relationship between the two hegemonic giants, beginning with what has become called the "Trade War." However, in the current context, the deterioration of this relationship is leading many analysts to identify a situation that goes beyond trade relations, reaching a situation worse than that seen during the bipolar conflict between the United States and the Soviet Union. Are we in a new Cold War? Some people already consider this speculation as fact. Jeffrey Sachs, for example, is one of them. For the American economist, this new conflict is not only a reality but also a "global threat greater than coronavirus."

Biden's election pointed to a substantial change in the question of the relationship between the two great powers. The war in Ukraine made dialogue practically impossible. As a matter of fact, will the United States and Russia maintain business relationships in the future? Also, how will U.S.–China relations evolve?

VIII. Science and health issues: Appreciation of scientists and health professionals

One consequence of the pandemic is obviously the treatment of the health sector, not only in developed countries (as the North American case) as well as in developing countries (as is our case).

Appreciation of science will be a consequence of Covid-19. It is clear that the world must be prepared to face new crises. The role of the WHO should be revisited.

Certainly, one of the responses to the Covid-19 crisis that became clear was the issue of technology. Many doctors, unable to see their patients in their office, have used telemedicine. The number of Brazilian companies that offer its use as an extra benefit has also grown. Many companies have done this for their employees. In the cargo transport sector, it is an additional reality. The testimonials from users that have used telemedicine have been very positive and encouraging. At Albert Einstein hospital in São Paulo, one of its doctors, Carlos Pedrotti, through teleconsultation, has started seeing 1.5 million people.

McKinsey estimates that revenues from medical care through telemedicine, pharmacy, wearable devices and others will increase from US\$350 billion over last year to US\$600 billion by 2024. Sectors of the US\$3.6 trillion health care market in the United States are ready for digital transformation. The same is true in China, Europe and many other places where doctors practice their craft.

Parallel to telemedicine, the market had already been developing as one of the main tools in offering telemonitoring systems that allow the patient to be followed at a distance. Among many medium-sized companies that have started their activities in recent years is the multinational giant Siemens. Thus, everything leads us to believe that this sector will grow exceptionally fast.

It is to be imagined that, in any case, we should have an appreciation of science, not only in the basic question of research directed toward the prevention of future pandemics, which many consider likely. We should be concerned with developing vaccines, but also devote resources to research into the emergence of new viruses. Right now, instead of seeing doctors face-to-face it's possible to have on-line appointments.

IX. Future direction of public and private investments in Brazil and worldwide

As a consequence of the crisis, it became evident the need to redirect public and private investments to the health sector, also because of its great correlation with sanitation in Brazilian cities. To demand confinement of residents in precarious conditions with large numbers of family members inhabiting shacks of 20–30 square meters was asking for the impossible. This raises the issue of urban planning, particularly regarding slums, which must be given special attention, in the sense of transforming them into a decent living environment, which, undoubtedly, could have a positive effect on crime. Investments in sanitation are essential.

This situation was not faced exclusively by Brazil, but also in many countries, especially in poor countries. Even in middle-income countries, the greatest loss of life occurred in poorer segments of the population, and especially among people of African descent and Latinos.

X. World and domestic economy: Its effects on international relations

Certainly, the impact on world economies in the short term will be severe. Even China, which had been showing high growth rates that benefited different countries, mainly suppliers of raw materials, will suffer a strong impact, which already project their growth for 2022 around 3.5 percent, the lowest in many years. Some activities that depend upon Chinese demand are already reflecting that situation, particularly commodities, agricultural as well as minerals like iron ore.

Like many countries with less weight in international trade, Brazil will suffer an impact on its balance of trade due to the drop in consumption of commodities in major client countries, as is the case of China. In the medium term, perhaps we may benefit, if the country is structured to receive foreign investment and apply resources in sectors in which we will be competitive due to the natural advantages we offer, not only by the decrease in exports but also the increase of imported goods and services.

It was once again evident with the Covid-19 crisis that in critical situations that the country experienced, the lack of education in its broadest sense is a factor that causes enormous distortions, with an interface in citizenship, social responsibility and respect for measures woven for the benefit of the population. The rebelliousness against social isolation and gradually opening to different activities is notorious.

It is worthwhile here to bring into discussion a topic that has been raised by many economists and politicians around the world (including Eduardo Suplicy—former senator of Brazil). A respected voice on the world stage, Kenneth Rogoff, Harvard University professor and former chief economist at the IMF, asked about the issue of minimum income:

I am all for it in this situation and also in the future, if the country can afford it. Income transfer to help the poor was an idea advocated by economists like Milton Friedman and James Tobin, both Nobel laureates. The main thing now is to take care of people's lives and then try to create the conditions for them to get back to work.

He also suggested attention to people who are in debt and help for small businesses.

In the Brazilian case, it was clear that the improvement seen in different sectors of the economy was mainly due to the financial flow made available to the unemployed and self-employed professionals. In December 2022 the support of the so-called *Auxílio Emergencial* will end, and the question is if the country will have the financial conditions to continue funding those groups, and without yet being able to consistently define a minimum developmental progress, with the necessary funding. At the end of October the candidate for reelection, Jair Bolsonaro, announced that the "renda minima" will be maintained for 2023. Lula also confirmed his position of total accordance in maintaining *Auxilio Brasil* during his four-year term. The question always present is how such expenses will be covered without fueling inflation.

In the short term, the government support programs released resources— as the support to the unemployed and self-employed to mitigate the effects of the pandemic in the country.

The reaction was gradual and differentiated by activity sectors.

As for investors, as mentioned earlier, we will have continued risk aversion due mostly to the external situation, and it will take some time for confidence numbers to be restored, even with asset prices at a much more realistic level, without the euphoria that mainly characterized the second half of 2019.

Further down the line, when the worst is over, and the social effects have been addressed, affected by the 2022 elections, we will have to start a program of fiscal consolidation, as the government's accounts were strongly impacted by the support programs.

XI. *Future being written*

The world will not be the same after the new coronavirus. It makes sense to transcribe, below, a brilliant article by Henry Kissinger, and published in the *Wall Street Journal*. From his experience and wisdom of many years on the international scene, I believe his authority is unquestionable.

From that article, we could underline the following points:

1) It is essential to break down divisions in countries to overcome obstacles unprecedented in their magnitude and global character. Sustaining public trust is basic to social solidarity among societies in the determined pursuit of peace and stability.

2) The institutions will see that they have failed. Regardless of their judgment, the truth is that the world will never be the same. It is no use looking at the past, but rather looking at what must be done for a new world relationship.

3) World leaders should not tackle the crisis on an individual basis, but recognize its devastating effect across borders, because the virus does not respect boundaries. This will require the United States to seek solutions with a vision of global collaboration. When looking at the Marshall Plan and Manhattan Project as a reference, three arrangements emerge to consider:

a.   Developing a vaccine with global resilience for infectious diseases. Measures should be taken to improve the protection of the most vulnerable population;

b.   Seek healing for the wounds of the world economy, for the lessons of the 2008 crisis to serve as an example, and avoid chaos;

c.   Safeguard the principles of world order. It is no longer a case of protecting the people from an external enemy. The pandemic has recreated countries with medieval barriers that are not the solution. We must balance power with the legitimacy of seeking solutions together. Reconstruction is the word!

BRAZILIAN FOREIGN TRADE FIGURES IN 2022

1.   In the year to September, Brazilian exports are 18.4 percent above the same period in 2021.

2.   Trade flow is 23.6 percent above the same period in 2021.

3.   Brazilian exports reached US$ 254 billion. Historical record for the period.

4.   The trade surplus (exports–imports) accumulated in the period was US$ 48 billion.

5.   Brazil exported to Asia (excluding China and the Middle East) US$ 36.5 billion. The value is almost the same exported in the period to the European Union (US$ 38.6 billion).

6.   Brazil exported more to ASEAN member countries (Brunei Darussalam, Cambodia, Singapore, Philippines, Indonesia, Laos, Malaysia, Myanmar, Thailand and Vietnam) than to Mercosur.

7.   The projected value for exports in 2022 is US$ 330 billion. If confirmed, it will be a historic record.

8.   The projected value for current trade in 2022 is US$ 605 billion. If confirmed, it will be a historic record.

9.   In comparison with the same period last year, Brazil shows growth in transactions with 19 of its 20 main export destinations.

Source: Brazilian Trade Balance (Jan.–Sep. 2022). SECEX-ME.

THE WAR IN UKRAINE AND
A DEVASTATED WORLD

As I finished writing an additional chapter for this book in December 2022, the devastating effects of the Russian invasion of Ukraine were more visible, as Vladimir Putin's "Special Military Operation" extended far beyond what most experts expected did not come to the quick conclusion most observers expected. The Russian aggressors were surprised by the determined resistance offered by the brave Ukrainians, led by President Volodymyr Zelenskyy, and by the degree of support by the West. The outcome of this conflict is still unclear, but, however it may turn out, some thoughts may be considered, as a basis for reflection, including the strong reactions of different players. What initially was expected to be an easy win for the Russians became more difficult and complex, and a long war prevailed.

As economist Kenneth Rogoff noted, the "peace bonus" may well be over. In effect, there have been many localized conflicts in the decades following World War II, but nothing comparable to the war in Ukraine.

We are living through a period that may be a turning point in history and international politics, not to mention possible developments including growing instability in the relations between Western countries, with Russia, and China. How will Brazil and Latin America be affected?

The economic sanctions imposed on Russia by Western countries have been a bitter medicine, with painful consequences for the rest of the world. It was the price to pay for our appreciation and respect for democracy and the rule of law. How long are these sanctions going to hold and what will be the permanent consequences? It is already clear at the short term: high rates of inflation due to scarcity of certain goods and the impact in economic growth.

The rebuilding of multilateralism, so important for the West after the damage done by the Trump administration, will suffer new setbacks? Will globalization suffer the consequences? According to Pierre-Olivier Gourinchas, IMF chief economist, the process of de-globalization that was already in place even before the Covid-19 epidemic strengthened after the war in Ukraine. Will we see a re-globalization? On what terms?

As never before, the Western world united itself in solidarity to condemn the attack on Ukraine and has been supplying the country with armament, as well as material and financial resources.

The UNHCR—with a long history of support for displaced people and refugees—noted the remarkable support and hospitality of neighboring peoples, especially Poland. Right now, over 100,000 people are considered refugees or displaced persons.

Another consequence has been the solidarity among countries that are part of the European Union and the strengthening of the North Atlantic Treaty Organization.

China's support for Putin, as expressed by Xi Jinping, surprised the world and may have a material economic and financial impact as a function of the geopolitics of global leadership.

At the outset of the invasion Russian foreign minister Sergei Lavrov stated that "there must be a redistribution of world power, whatever the costs." He did not, indeed, discard the risk of a third world war and the use of nuclear weapons. One should ask: is the insanity of authoritarian regimes pushing the world back to a darker period?

This war brings back the potential of, at a minimum, a cold war and the isolation of Russia from the Western world, at a critical moment for global cooperation against climate change.

Military spending is growing, especially in Germany, with a threefold increase in their military budget, but also in other Western European powers. The U.S. Congress has budgeted US$ 813 billion for defense in 2022, US$ 40 billion of which to homeland defense. In December 2022, Japan announced a planned doubling in defense expenditures in line with the country's changed security strategy.

The exodus of Ukrainian refugees appears to be probably the largest forced displacement of people of the modern era, estimated around 10 percent of the country's prewar population and with a high percentage of children. So far most of them have been absorbed by neighboring countries, combined with certain emerging countries. Will they ever return to their devastated homeland? What will be the cost of reconstructing Ukraine? The preliminary costs for reconstructing Ukraine will be around US$ 600 billion, but the war continues. Where will the money come from? Some politicians have suggested a Marshall Plan like the one introduced after the end of World War II. In meantime, Volodymyr Zelenskyy, president of Ukraine, had a successful trip to the United States in December 2022 and received standing ovation by Congress and financial support of nearly US$2 billion in assistance.

The goals of the United States, according to Defense Secretary Lloyd Austin, were to degrade Russia's military potential and strengthen Ukraine's. "[The United States] wanted to see Russia weakened to the degree that it can't repeat what was done in invading Ukraine."

After this introduction, it may be worthwhile to assess the state of the world economy more specifically:

1. Points in common—Declines in previously forecasted growth in European economies and a risk of recession in certain countries. Inflation is present, to a bigger or lesser extent, across world economies. In the United States the inflation rate was already at a 40-year peak before the war. In the United Kingdom the cost of natural gas for domestic use has already risen to a point that weakened Prime Minister Boris Johnson's position and forced him to resign. He has been replaced by Liz Truss, who resigned less than two months later. Then Rishi Sunak was selected to continue to implement conservative economic policies.

2. However, even though the war is having some influence on U.S. equity markets, it has not been as consequential as the crisis of 2020, when the WHO recognized the Covid-19 pandemic. Inflation is reducing purchasing power. The evolution of prices and the actions by the Federal Reserve will be decisive. The perception arose that the Fed did not raise rates fast enough when the first signs of inflation arose, and may be forced to overcompensate, due to continuously rising prices.

3. Supply chain bottlenecks have had a short-term impact on prices. Some countries will reconsider their supply channels, favoring domestic suppliers or those from their zones of influence, despite higher short-term production costs. This is what happened to pharma and medicinal supplies during the Covid-19 pandemic. Consequently, there will be pressure on wages, feeding inflation. It will not decrease quickly and may last for a long time. Some analysts project no respite in lower inflation any sooner than 2025.

Long sanctions may cause the breakdown of global supply chains. Prolonged sanctions can impose costs not only on their targets but also on third parties. This may be an opportunity, however, for Latin America to deepen integration into global supply chains and may play a key role in offsetting the rise in raw materials' prices.

Larry Fink, CEO of BlackRock, one of the world's largest fund managers, is one of the many world leaders who have stated that the conflict-induced reorganization of global supply chains may benefit Latin American countries.

José Manuel Durão, former president of the European Commission, among others, also gave the same indication.

The U.S. undersecretary of State for Economic Growth, Energy and the Environment, Mr. José Fernandez, indicated that Brazil may become a regional leader in the process of reorganization of global supply chains. Immunizer production capacity makes Brazil a strategic partner of the United States. The Inter-American Development Bank ranked Brazil as number one in terms of partnership between private and public sector.

In November 2022 for the first time the presidency of the bank will be held by a Brazilian, economist Ilan Goldfajn, former president of the Brazilian Central Bank.

Brazil's balance of current transactions, favorably influenced by the large trade surplus, may reach a positive balance for the first time after 15 years of deficits. Brazilian foreign exchange reserves topped US$ 362 billion in December 2021.

Interesting discussions are taking place on who could benefit from the European energy crisis, as several energy-intensive players such as aluminum and steel companies may have to shut down their production given extremely high energy prices. In one meeting, an investor mentioned Brazil as a good investment option in such a scenario. A competitive advantage for Brazil is the availability of different sources of renewable energy: solar, wind, hydropower and bioenergy.

4. Higher inflation is the mortal enemy of efforts to reduce inequality and in Brazil will affect 13 million people who were about to cross the poverty line. Unfortunately, inequality is likely to rise.

   Undoubtedly an auspicious fact is that despite all the difficulties the entrepreneurial spirit was intact.

5. Brazilian agriculture may benefit from the crisis, but higher fertilizer prices may impact the cost of agricultural production, until their supply normalizes or until we find ways to import from alternative suppliers.

6. Very bullish view for Brazil. Investors were either neutral or overweight but with clear intentions to increase exposure. Brazil looks attractive compared with other emerging markets and even with other developed economies. It is all about macro. Inflation, interest rates, currency, fiscal policy and recent upward revisions of GDP were the key topics.

Certainly, the Brazilian elite should be paying attention to the external scenario that is bound to affect us. More than ever, we should be trying to maneuver Brazil into a more favorable position in the new configuration of international politics. Certainly, with a minimum of good sense, we should be able to take advantage of the new economic and financial conditions after total isolation of Russia implies paying a significant price. Cutting all channels of communication seems questionable and a dialogue should be reestablished.

As we were adding the finishing touches to this manuscript we were struck by the news of the passing of Edson Arantes do Nascimento, better known as Pelé. Well known all over the world as the greatest footballer of all time, he was an outstanding goodwill ambassador for Brazil, the "king of soccer." He seems to embody the idea that with talent, effort and grace Brazilians could do great things, despite a disadvantaged background. He will be sorely missed.

Perhaps, his funeral was one of the deepest public demonstrations in Pelé's 24-hour wake. It was estimated that 230,000 people filed through the Santos Stadium (Pelé made Santos Futebol Clube famous around the world), waiting up to four hours for a final farewell.

We should recognize our virtues as well as our blemishes, but not think of ourselves as losers. That has been the tone of my 2021 book:

Brazil should not be afraid of the world!

PHOTOGRAPHS

Greeting speech during President Jimmy Carter's visit to São Paulo, on 21 January 1997, with his autograph.

1. Latin America Business Council event at the São Paulo Club with José Ermírio de Moraes, Jimmy Carter and Rosalynn Carter.

2. Meeting of the Latin American Business Council at Copacabana Palace with former presidents: Julio Maria Sanguinetti (Uruguay), Fernando Henrique Cardoso (Brazil) and Raul Cubas (Paraguay).

3. Meeting in Brasilia during Fernando Henrique Cardoso's presidency with Fernando Henrique Cardoso, Manuel Feliú (former president of the Chilean Chapter of CEAL), Pedro Piva, Luís Cesar Fernandes, Aloisio Araujo and Daniel Klabin.

4. Bill Clinton on his first visit to Brazil after leaving the presidency—with Luiz Felipe Lampreia (then chancellor) and Thomas Marc Larty (U.S. special envoy for Latin America).

5. Meeting of Foro Iberoamerica at the Government Palace in Campos do Jordão with Gustavo Cisneros and Felipe Gonzales.

6. Iberoamerica Forum meeting in Campos do Jordão with Carlos Slim, Paolo Rocca and Guilherme de La Dehesa.

7. Meeting at Keidanren in Tokyo with Cacilda Teixeira da Costa and Sonia Simão.

8. Meeting in São Paulo with Octavio Frias and Henry Kissinger.

9. Roberto Teixeira da Costa during Fernando Henrique Cardoso's visit to Shanghai (1995).

10. Visit to Embraco in China with Ernesto Heinzelmann, Hugo Miguel Echenique and Aloizio Araujo.

11. Meeting of the Council of the Americas in Washington with George Bush.

12. Dinner in São Paulo with Robert Zoellick (United States secretary of Foreign Policy).

13. Latin America Business Council Meeting (during the presidency of Roberto Teixeira da Costa) at the Alvorada Palace in Brasilia (1980) with the presidents of the Republic of the region.

14. Induction of President Ricardo Lagos (Chile).

15. Meeting of the Iberoamerican General Secretariat in Madrid with King Felipe VI.

16. CEAL's Emeritus Councilor title delivered in Foz do Iguaçu.

17. Dinner at CEAL with Alberto Fujimori and Aluizio Araujo (1996).

18. Visit to the Venezuelan refugee camp in Boa Vista (RR) in the company of the members of the Mobilizing Committee of the UN Agency for Refugees (UNHCR), May 2019.

19. Business Forum and *Ministerial* Summit of the Americas *in Cartagena* (1996).

ABOUT THE AUTHOR

During my previous performance as director of an investment bank, and later as vice president in charge of BIB (later, with the conglomeration of the financial system, it became part of Unibanco) I kept frequent contact with my international counterparts.

Acting in Capital Markets

It was a rich experience, as we simultaneously promoted Brazil and the opportunities in the stock market and represented a newly created financial institution, an investment bank BIB. Such experience was certainly crucial to my appointment to form Comissão de Valores Mobiliarios (Brazilian SEC) and be its first president.

Immediately after leaving the presidency of CVM—Securities and Exchange Commission of Brazil (Dec/1979), the subject of international relations began to occupy a growing space in my agenda. Upon returning to São Paulo, I became CEO of Brasilpar, a pioneer in the venture capital area.

Even so, this coexistence with international developments was important for my professional experience, gaining insight into our country from an external perspective. My experience has already resulted in three books on capital markets.[1] I emphasize the little information about Brazil and a curiosity in some cases to have more knowledge about our market, institutions, with their positive as well as negative aspects.

Since then, the distancing of the Brazilian financial and industrial elite from the international scene had attracted my attention. With a closed economy that did not create incentives for external investments, whether by industrial investors or even by corporations. It was not attractive for them to go to foreign markets due to lack of knowledge and low-capacity building

---

1 They are: (i) *Brazil's Experience in Creating a Capital Market* (Bovespa, 1985); (ii) *Capital Markets: A 50-year Trajectory* (São Paulo: Official Press of the Estado de São Paulo, 2006); and (iii) *Worth it! Capital Markets: Past, Present and Future* (Ed. FGV, 2018).

from an administrative and financial point of view. The insufficient scale of our industrial production did not create foreign sales potential, as well as, when our products were competitive, we did not guarantee the expected return. In a few cases, this incursion abroad happened when crises in the domestic market forced the industrialists to look abroad. For obvious reasons, it was the neighboring countries that aroused the most interest.

That situation has motivated my involvement in different institutions where the main purpose was to motivate Brazilians to be more active in different markets around the world.

Creation of the Latin American Business Council (Ceal)

Ceal was an initiative of Argentinean businessmen, led by Ricardo Esteves, who felt the need for a greater approximation between his Argentinean peers and those of our country. We were foreseeing the possibilities of Mercosur, and the contacts that existed between them were very precarious.

Thus, it seemed appropriate to create an association of businesspeople that would bring us together and allow periodic meetings to exchange business information, reports of institutional experiences, exploring success stories of public and administrative–financial policies that would serve for mutual inspiration.

The first president of the Brazilian Chapter was Paulo Villares (we were organized in the form of chapters) after successive assemblies in Buenos Aires and Rio, when it was decided to formalize the association.

Following the presidency of Paulo Villares, I was invited to preside over the Brazilian Chapter, which I held continuously for a period of eight years, the last two years of which I accumulated with the presidency of the international chapter.

Except for Mexico, because of its geographic proximity to the United States and its specific characteristics, and Chile (more open), I observed that the region's entrepreneurs were, as well, very focused on their respective markets, although due to their Hispanic background, in many cases they had a greater proximity to each other (common language) and perhaps a greater proximity with Europe, particularly Spain.

I also realized that the sovereignty issue, among other factors, did not allow them to accept Brazilian leadership.

Ceal is still active, but it is having to adapt to the new circumstances of the world economy, where communication facilities dispense with the need for direct contacts. Today, as we all know, we live in an inverse situation: too much information. The biggest problem is to separate the useful information, not to mention the "Fake News."

Creation of Brazilian Center for International Relations (CEBRI)

The formation of CEBRI was also a school of learning as to the need to be equipped to internally discuss themes about our country's relationship with the rest of the world, as well as, about the difficulties of engaging Brazilian businessmen in the discussion and debates related to the insertion of Brazil in the international scenario and its responsibility to businessmen.

In our region, we were at a disadvantage vis-à-vis Argentina and Chile, which had think tanks to discuss foreign policy many years before we got organized. (In the case of Chile, for example, when Fernando Henrique Cardoso was in exile in the Andean country, its International Relations Council already existed, while the Argentine Council on International Relations—CARI—had already been formed since 1978.)

Right now, it is a reality as a think tank that has a large number of participants, holding frequent meetings related to international relations as well as publishing policy papers.

Mercosur European Union Business Forum (MEBF)

When I finished my term at Ceal, Ambassador Roberto Abdenur, then our representative in Germany, was contacted by the president of the German Confederation of Industries, Hans-Olaf Henkel, who proposed the creation of business forum parallel to the EU–Mercosur negotiations. I was consulted about coordinating the Brazilian side in a possible association, counting on the strong support of the Argentinean oil businessman, Carlos Bulgheroni. We then created an association along the lines of the Transatlantic Dialogue, which brought North American and European businessmen together for the commercial alliance between the European Union and the United States, and which was called the MEBF.

This invitation was made official by Ambassador José Botafogo Gonçalves, at the time head of the Ministry of Development, Industry and Trade, and since then, therefore for more than 20 years, this trade agreement has been under discussion, which unfortunately has not yet become viable, despite several diplomatic attempts in different forums. My counterpart on the European side was the president of BASF, Jürgen Strube, with whom I had a very productive relationship, and we held several meetings, including at BASF headquarters.

Later, in the coordination of the Brazilian side of the MEBF passed to several representative entrepreneurs of the industrial sector such as: Luiz Fernando Furlan, Ingo Plöger and Carlos Mariani. On the governmental side, my companions in this endeavor were Ambassador Roberto Jaguaribe, who occupied several embassies, including the Brazilian Trade and Investment Promotion Agency (Apex).

Foro Iberoamérica

Also inspired by Ricardo Esteves, and by Mexican writer Carlos Fuentes, the Foro was an initiative to bring together politicians, writers and businesspeople from "Iberoamerica," i.e., Spanish- and Portuguese-speaking communities from Iberia and America. It held annual meetings alternating between Europe and Latin America and I was privileged to participate in its discussions and exchanges of ideas. The Foro was discontinued in July 2022.

International Analysis Group (Gacint) and Institute of International Relations (IRI)

Invited by Ambassador Celso Lafer, and sociologist Gilberto Dupas, I became a member of the International Analysis Group (Gacint) linked to the International Relations Institute (IRI) of the USP of which I also participate as a member of its collegiate advisor.

Gacint holds periodic meetings on the campus of the USP, always with topics related to the international scenario and its implications for our country. It has been a laboratory for discussions of topics of institutional, political and economic interest.

In 2022, I was elected as member of the Board of orientation of IRI.

IAD

To finish this listing of institutions to which I have been connected, I must mention the IAD in Washington. The Dialogue, which had among its founders, besides other expressive world leaders, President Fernando Henrique Cardoso, is recognized for its interest in bringing the United States closer to Latin American issues and interests. It was founded in 1982 and today has more than 100 members from 23 countries in the Americas.

I have been part of its board at three different times, completing another term in 2023. We have two council meetings a year, but the Dialogue also holds a series of weekly meetings always trying to bring up issues that are sensitive to our region and its relationship not only with the United States, but also among the rest. The presence of the Central American theme has always been present.

INDEX

Printed in the USA
CPSIA information can be obtained
at www.ICGtesting.com
JSHW021609110923
48262JS00001B/6